Essential Hist

Rome at

Essential Histories

Rome at War AD 293–696

Michael Whitby

OSPREY
PUBLISHING

First published in Great Britain in 2002 by Osprey Publishing,
Elms Court, Chapel Way, Botley, Oxford OX2 9LP, UK
Email: info@ospreypublishing.com

ISBN 1 84176 359 4

Editor: Rebecca Cullen
Design: Ken Vail Graphic Design, Cambridge, UK
Cartography by The Map Studio
Index by David Ballheimer
Picture research by Image Select International
Origination by Grasmere Digital Imaging, Leeds, UK
Printed and bound in China by L. Rex Printing Company Ltd.

02 03 04 05 06   10 9 8 7 6 5 4 3 2 1

For a complete list of titles available from Osprey Publishing
please contact:

Osprey Direct UK, PO Box 140,
Wellingborough, Northants, NN8 2FA, UK.
Email: info@ospreydirect.co.uk

Osprey Direct USA, c/o MBI Publishing,
PO Box 1, 729 Prospect Ave,
Osceola, WI 54020, USA.
Email: info@ospreydirectusa.com

www.ospreypublishing.com

Contents

Introduction

In the early third century AD the Roman Empire stretched from Scotland to the Sahara and to the northern River Tigris – an enormous imperial enterprise and the most powerful state in the world. Four centuries later the Empire had shrunk to consist of Anatolia, the Aegean fringes of the Balkans and limited territories in Italy around Rome and Ravenna. Still strong in Mediterranean terms, it was forced to confront and interact with a variety of new powers. To the east Arabs, inspired by Islam, had overrun the Levant and Egypt, as well as the Persian kingdom. More than a millennium of conflict between Islamic east and Christian west was introduced as Arab warriors pushed westwards through North Africa and into Spain and regularly raided towards Constantinople. Slav tribes established themselves throughout much of

the Balkans, with specific leaders emerging in certain areas: Bulgars in the north-east, Serbs and Croats in the north-west. In Italy the Lombard kingdom, based in the Po valley, fragmented authority in the peninsula, and so it remained until reunification in the 19th century. Franks controlled Gaul, though it was usually split between different branches of the ruling Merovingian dynasty. In the Iberian peninsula the Visigoths had established authority, sometimes tenuously, over the groups who had settled during the fifth century; however, their switch from Arian to Nicene Christianity in the seventh

The Emperor Theodosius and his family receive tokens of submission from barbarians while seated in the imperial box at the hippodrome. From the base of the obelisk at the Hippodrome in Constantinople. (Ancient Art and Architecture)

century provided a force for unity which would survive centuries of conflict with Muslim invaders. The British Isles presented another mosaic, with Saxons increasingly dominant in the south and east, Britons holding on in the west, and rival Pictish and Scottish kingdoms in control of southern Scotland. Here again religion offered hope for future unity, with the Saxons progressively converted through the Roman mission based at Canterbury and the Celtic Church, which was dominant in Ireland, Scotland and the north-west, then reconciled with Roman traditions.

By the end of the seventh century many of the important elements of the modern European political landscape were in place, or at least in evidence, but the stages whereby Roman hegemony fragmented are complex. It is essential, above all, to remember that there was nothing inevitable about this process: Europe did not have to be organised into the territorial units and dominated by the national groups with which we are familiar today. 'Decline and fall' has been a powerful model for analysing this transition, from the composition of Edward Gibbon's masterwork in the late eighteenth century, and before. But the vitality of the Roman system – especially when reinvigorated by Christianity – the commitment of peoples to the Roman ideal, and the sheer power of Roman arms also need to be stressed in opposition to this analysis.

Identification of turning points is an understandable temptation, and acceptable provided that the qualifications for each particular date are not forgotten. The conversion of Constantine to Christianity in AD 312 initiated the Empire's transformation from polytheism to Christianity, and prompted the development of the Church as a powerful and wealthy institution. For some scholars the Church was yet one more substantial group of idle mouths for Roman tax-payers to support, with unfortunate long-term consequences, but the Church also served imperial goals beyond the frontiers and reinforced loyalties within. In 363 Julian's grand invasion of Persia ended in death for him and near disaster for the Roman army,

Bronze head of Constantine with eyes characteristically gazing to heaven. (Ancient Art and Architecture)

but the setback ushered in 140 years of almost unbroken peace in the eastern Empire. In 378 the eastern emperor Valens was killed in battle at Adrianople in Thrace, and many of his Gothic opponents had to be allocated lands for settlement, but thereafter successive eastern emperors generally managed the 'Gothic problem' to their advantage. When the last sole Roman ruler Theodosius I died in 395, the Empire was split between his young sons, and emperors ceased to campaign regularly in person, but such divisions had occurred in the past, often beneficially, and there were advantages in withdrawing the emperor from the battlefield. 'Immortal' Rome was captured by Alaric's Visigoths in AD 410, but it had long ceased to be an imperial capital, so the event was largely of symbolic importance: Augustine in Africa wrote *City of God* to demonstrate the superiority of the heavenly over the terrestrial city, but in Italy the Visigoths withdrew and emperors continued to rule from Ravenna. In the 440s Attila challenged imperial authority – in both east and west, threatening even to reduce emperors to vassal status – but his Hunnic federation disintegrated after his death in 453 so that within a decade his heirs were seeking Roman help. In 476 the last Roman emperor in the western Empire was deposed by a 'barbarian' general, but the authority of the eastern emperor was still acknowledged. A western consul was annually nominated to share the chief titular magistracy with eastern colleagues, and under Theoderic the Ostrogoth a regime, which carefully maintained a Gotho-Roman façade dominated the western Mediterranean from Ravenna.

Individually the significance of each of these 'key' dates must be qualified, but

> One of the more accurate assessments of the Empire's demise occurs in a conversation between Jews in prison at Carthage in the 630s. They discuss the state of the Empire and the news of a new prophet among the Saracens in terms of the vision of Empire in the Book of Daniel (Doctrine of the Newly-baptised Jacob 3.8).
>
> 'Jacob asked him: "What do you think of the state of Romania? Does it stand as once, or has it been diminished?"
>
> Justus replied uncertainly, "Even if it has been somewhat diminished, we hope that it will rise again."
>
> But Jacob convinced him, "We see the nations believing in Christ and the fourth beast has fallen and is being torn in pieces by the nations, that the ten horns may prevail."'

cumulatively they contributed to diminishing imperial authority, undermining the fiscal and military structures which permitted the imperial machine to function. By the late fifth century an emperor had become irrelevant in the western Mediterranean, although the eastern ruler was accepted as a figurehead by some. The eastern Empire's continuing power was revealed by its ability to organise the reconquest of the Vandal and Ostrogothic kingdoms, which extended to the recovery of parts of Spain and the exercise of intermittent influence in Gaul. Even if the cumulative impact of recurrent bubonic plague and the demands of western warfare left the Empire economically and militarily weaker in AD 600 than it had been in AD 500, in comparative terms it might have been stronger, since its greatest rival, the Persian kingdom, also suffered heavily during a century of conflict; its then ruler, Khusro II, had only secured the throne with Roman help. In the early seventh century internal dissension and foreign invasion seemed to have forced the Romans to the brink of destruction, symbolised by the arrival of a Persian army on the Bosporus and its co-operation with the Avar Chagan in the AD 626 attack on Constantinople. But the city and its Empire survived: within two years Heraclius had defeated the Persians, and overseen the installation of friendly rulers on the Persian throne, including, briefly, the Christian Shahvaraz; and during the 630s the Avar federation began to disintegrate as the reduced prestige of its leader permitted subordinate tribes to assert their independence. For the eastern Empire the decisive blow came out of the blue when the new religion of Islam transformed long-standing manageable neighbours into a potent adversary.

Chronology

226	Ardashir overthrows Parthian dynasty.
235	Murder of Severus Alexander by troops.
243/4	Gordian defeated by Shapur I of Persia.
251	Death of Decius in battle against Goths.
260	Defeat and capture of Valerian by Persians. Franks invade Gaul; Alamanni invade Italy; revolts in Balkans.
261–68	Odaenathus of Palmyra takes control of eastern provinces.
262–67	Goths invade Asia Minor.
271	Aurelian withdraws Romans from Dacia. Circuit of walls built for Rome.
272	Aurelian defeats Palmyra.
275	Murder of Aurelian.
284	Accession of Diocletian.
293	Tetrarchy with Maximian as co-Augustus and Constantius and Galerius as Caesars.
305	Abdication of Diocletian and Maximian.
312	Constantine captures Rome after battle of Milvian Bridge.
324	Constantine defeats Licinius and becomes sole emperor.
337	Death of Constantine at start of campaign against Persia.
353	Constantius II defeats usurper Magnentius and reunifies Empire.
355	Julian co-opted by Constantius as Caesar.
357	Julian defeats Alamanni at Strasburg.
361	Death of Constantius.
363	Julian's invasion of Persia and death.
376	Goths cross the Danube.
378	Defeat and death of Valens at Adrianople (Edirne).
382	Theodosius settles Goths in Balkans as federates.
394	Theodosius defeats usurper Eugenius and reunifies Empire.
395	Death of Theodosius; Empire divided between Arcadius and Honorius.
406	German tribes breach Rhine frontier.
408	Stilicho executed.
410	Sack of Rome by Alaric and Visigoths.
418	Establishment of Visigoths in Aquitania.
429	Vandals cross into Africa.
445	Attila becomes sole ruler of Huns.
451	Attila invades Gaul; defeated at Catalaunian Plains (near Troyes).
453	Death of Attila.
455	Vandals sack Rome.
476	Odoacer deposes Romulus Augustulus, the last western emperor.
493	Theoderic captures Ravenna and kills Odoacer.
502	Kavadh invades eastern provinces and captures Amida (Diyarbakir).
505	Truce on eastern frontier; construction of Dara starts.
507	Clovis and Franks defeat Visigoths at Vouillé.
527	Renewed warfare in east. Accession of Justinian.
532	'Endless Peace' with Persia.
533	Belisarius defeats Vandals and recovers Africa.
540	Belisarius enters Ravenna and ends Ostrogothic kingdom. Khusro I invades eastern provinces and captures Antioch.
542	Arrival of bubonic plague.
546	Totila recaptures Rome.
552	Narses defeats and kills Totila at Busta Gallorum.
562	50 Years Peace with Persia.
568	Lombards invade Italy.
572	Justin II launches new war on eastern frontier.
578/9	Avar invasions of Balkans start.
586/7	Slav raids reach Athens and Corinth.
591	Termination of war with Persia.

602	Revolt of Balkan army and overthrow of Maurice.
610	Heraclius captures Constantinople and kills Phocas.
614	Persians capture Jerusalem.
622	Muhammad leaves Medina (*Hijra*).
626	Avars besiege Constantinople, with Persian support.
627	Heraclius defeats Persians at Nineveh.
632	Death of Muhammad.
636	Arabs defeat Romans at River Yarmuk.
638	Arabs capture Jerusalem.
639	Arabs attack Egypt.
642	Arabs capture Alexandria.
651	Death of Yazdgard III, last Sassanid ruler.
661	Mu'awiyah becomes Caliph at Damascus.

Controlling the empire

Marking boundaries

The centuries of conflict covered in this volume saw the Romans pitted against enemies in three main sectors: along the Rhine against the Alamanni, Franks and other Germanic tribes; on the Danube against first the Sarmatians and Goths, then the Hunnic tribes, and finally the Avars and manifold Slav groups; in Armenia and Mesopotamia the Sassanid Persians; eventually, towards the end of the period, Arab tribes erupted from the Arabian peninsula to sweep through the Levant. Since the Roman Empire was a military institution whose widespread control had been imposed by force, there was naturally a long history of conflict in each sector, even if the precise opponents were not always the same.

The Romans first campaigned on the Rhine in the 50s BC during Caesar's conquest of Gaul, although it was only a century later that the frontier stabilised along the river – once grander Roman visions to incorporate Germania were renounced. Temporary military installations were replaced in stone, permanent camps attracted settlements of veterans, traders and other camp-followers, and prosperous sites were honoured with colonial status, for example Colonia Agrippina (Cologne) and Moguntiacum (Mainz). Stability along the frontier required active defence, and there were major campaigns commanded by an emperor in the 90s (Domitian), 170s (Marcus Aurelius) and 230s (Severus Alexander).

The Rhine provided a partial barrier to tribal movement which the Romans could

Impressive defences reinforced Rome's psychological superiority along the frontiers. Taken from Trajan's column in Rome. (AKG London/Hilbich)

Troops crossing a river by pontoon bridge, from a section of Trajan's column. (AKG Berlin)

control through naval squadrons and by supervising recognised crossing-points. Beyond the Rhine were numerous tribal groups whose relationship with the Romans was not always hostile: tribesmen served in Roman armies, Roman garrisons had considerable wealth (by local standards) to spend on slaves, furs or basic foodstuffs, while the Romans were a source of luxury goods such as wine or spices. A symbiotic relationship could emerge: Romans wanted tribal manpower and supplies, while tribal leaders relied on Romans for the wealth and display goods to demonstrate superiority over their rank and file. A cyclical pattern to relations on the frontier can be seen: the Romans bolstered the authority of compliant leaders whose expanding following generated greater demands; when these became excessive, conflict ensued between Rome and a major tribal grouping; thereafter the cycle would begin again.

The second major European river frontier, along the Danube, was joined to the Rhine frontier by linear defences, which protected a triangle of territory to the south-east of Argentoratum (Strasburg), always a sensitive area. The Romans had reached the upper and middle Danube during the reign of Augustus (31 BC–AD 14), confirming their control over the hinterland in the face of massive rebellions in Pannonia and Illyricum; further downstream the Danube became the frontier during the first century AD. A process of consolidation similar to that on the Rhine got under way, but in this case the need to dominate the Dacian tribes of the lower Danube led to major campaigns across the river under Trajan (98–117) in the early second century and the creation of a new province within the arc of the Carpathian mountains.

In the eastern Empire the Romans encountered the Parthians during the first century BC, experiencing one of their worst defeats in 53 BC when three legions were annihilated at Carrhae (Harran) in Mesopotamia. Until the mid-first century AD,

Roman provinces c. AD 200–700

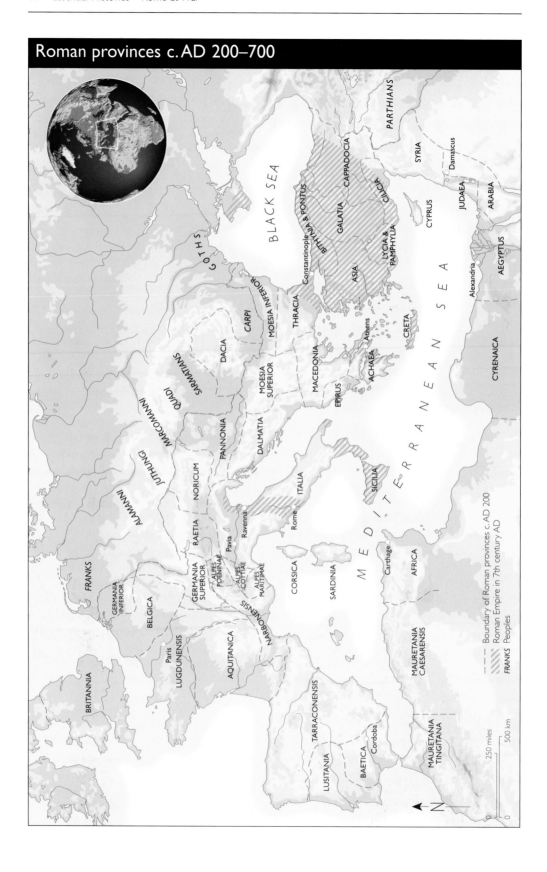

PARTHIANS

BLACK SEA

GOTHS

SARMATIANS

QUADI

MARCOMANNI

IUTHUNGI

ALMANNI

FRANKS

GERMANIA
INFERIOR

BELGICA

LUGDUNENSIS

Paris

BRITANNIA

AQUITANICA

NARBONENSIS

GERMANIA
SUPERIOR

ALPES
POENINAE

ALPES
COTTIAE

ALPES
MARITIMAE

RAETIA

NORICUM

PANNONIA

DACIA

CARPI

MOESIA INFERIOR

MOESIA
SUPERIOR

DALMATIA

ITALIA

Ravenna

Pavia

Rome

CORSICA

SARDINIA

SICILIA

THRACIA

MACEDONIA

EPIRUS

ACHAEA

Athens

CRETA

BITHYNIA & PONTUS

Constantinople

GALATIA

CAPPADOCIA

ASIA

LYCIA &
PAMPHYLIA

CILICIA

CYPRUS

SYRIA

Damascus

JUDAEA

ARABIA

AEGYPTUS

Alexandria

CYRENAICA

MEDITERRANEAN SEA

Carthage

AFRICA

MAURETANIA
CAESARENSIS

MAURETANIA
TINGITANA

TARRACONENSIS

LUSITANIA

BAETICA

Cordoba

Boundary of Roman provinces c. AD 200

Roman Empire in 7th century AD

FRANKS   Peoples

250 miles

500 km

N

small client kingdoms constituted buffer states for Roman territory in Anatolia and the Levant. Thereafter the upper and middle Euphrates provided a suitable line on which to base legionary positions – though, as along the European rivers, the Romans maintained a keen interest in events beyond. Between the River Euphrates and the Arabian Gulf, desert offered a reliable buffer zone, although tribes who knew how to operate in this inhospitable terrain troubled Roman lands to the west intermittently. For the Romans the east was the prestigious area for conflict, ideally for expansion, with the renown of Alexander the Great's achievements luring successive western rulers to emulation: in the early second century Trajan campaigned to the head of the Persian Gulf, briefly establishing a province in Mesopotamia; in the 160s Lucius Verus (161–9) fought energetically in lower Mesopotamia, and in the 190s Septimius Severus (193–211) again defeated the Parthians and annexed new territory.

A view along part of Hadrian's wall (showing Chester's fort), another defensive structure which combined protection and propaganda. (Ancient Art and Architecture)

North Africa, which the Romans gradually took over between the mid-second century BC and the mid-first century AD, resembled the southern portion of the eastern frontier. Desert, supplemented on occasion by linear barriers, played a significant part in marking the boundaries of Roman authority. Tribal instability could pose threats, though, as along the European frontiers; 'outsiders' were tied into the Roman system through military service and economic exchanges. The British Isles, which the Romans invaded in the first century AD, stands in contrast to the other major frontiers as a place where the Romans relied primarily on linear defences – the walls of Hadrian and Antoninus – to separate the untamed tribes of Caledonia from Roman areas.

It is ironic that the best-studied Roman defences – the salient between the Rhine and Danube in south-western Germany and the walls of north Britain – are not typical of Roman frontier areas overall. As a consequence, however, we may fail to understand how the frontiers operated. The traditional view is that frontiers were maintained to delimit and protect Roman territory by barring entry to foreigners. But

frontiers are now seen as zones of contact, as much as lines of exclusion: this is clearly true for the European river frontiers, and even in the case of an apparent barrier, scrutiny of the installations along Hadrian's Wall reveals its purpose was to control, but not prevent, movement. It is also argued that generals and emperors were more interested in the rewards of conquest than in routine defence of the Empire's inhabitants, and that from the military perspective the provinces more often required subjugation than protection. Exchanges across frontiers, the significance of military glory, and the preservation of law and order are all valid considerations, but the ideology of *pax Romana* was also important: emperors were believed to have a duty towards the civilian members of the Empire – or at least their performance of this role was an issue which might be picked up in speeches of praise or defamatory tracts.

Within the frontier Roman territory was divided into provinces, of which there were about 60 in the early third century AD. Most provincial governors were drawn from the senate, the council made up of former magistrates, which had considerable authority but little real power. Governors of frontier provinces with substantial armies were chosen from among former consuls (the most senior group within the senate) by the emperor. In the 'interior' provinces the governors' primary functions were to

A panel from Constantine's arch at Rome showing the emperor distributing largesse. This victory monument depicts the emperor's civilian virtues as well as his military triumphs. (AKG London/Pirozzi)

maintain imperial control and ensure the smooth collection of taxation. They suppressed brigandage (which subsisted at a low level in many parts of the Empire), regulated disputes between provincial cities and ensured their internal stability, and oversaw communications between the province and Rome, including the important annual expressions of allegiance to the emperor.

Taxes and trade

Taxation was the lifeblood of the Empire, which depended upon a regular cyclical flow of wealth. The areas of greatest consumption were Rome – where the imperial court and senatorial households spent lavishly – and the frontier armies whose salaries had to be paid to prevent the risk of mutiny. Most frontier provinces could not support the full costs of the legions based in them, and so tax surpluses had to be transferred from 'interior' regions, for example Spain or Asia Minor where the inhabitants generated cash to meet tax demands by selling produce: the Empire evolved quite a complex system which locked different areas together. The two most important taxes were a poll tax and a land tax. The former was simpler, although its coverage and rate varied. The latter was based on an assessment of land value as determined by agricultural use, for example arable as opposed to vineyard or pastureland, and was levied as a fixed percentage of the valuation. These taxes were not progressive, which meant that financial burdens fell more heavily on small-holders than grandees, who would also have greater influence to secure exemptions. In addition there were customs duties at both

imperial and provincial boundaries, and a 5 per cent tax for Roman citizens on inheritances and the freeing of slaves.

Movement of produce, as both trade and tax revenue, was an important aspect of the Empire's economic system. Massive amounts of grain from Egypt and other parts of North Africa, and of oil and wine from Spain, were transported to supply Rome as taxation or the produce of imperial estates; similarly senators' provincial estates supported their palatial households in the capital. Supplies for the army might also seem to be located within this command economy and to an extent they were, but the Vindolanda writing tablets, which preserve correspondence of an auxiliary cohort based in north Britain c. AD 100 reveal that army units were also supported by their own supply networks.

The best evidence for Roman trade inevitably relates to the exceptional needs of the elite, who had an enormous appetite for eastern 'luxuries': spices from eastern Africa, and silks, gems and spices from India. The eastern trade was a substantial enterprise; it enriched both the imperial exchequer through customs revenues and the middlemen whose profits were invested in Petra and Palmyra. The current view of the Roman economy, based in part on the increasing evidence from ship-wrecks, is that trade played a minor but significant role in the Empire's prosperity: trade in luxury items was the tip of an iceberg of local, intra-regional and inter-regional exchange which was greatly facilitated by the existence of the roads, ports and other installations established to service the crucial elements of the imperial system, namely the capital and the armies.

Overall, the Empire was prosperous during the first two centuries AD, as can be seen from the archaeological remains of provincial cities where local elites competed to beautify their home towns. Wealth did flow out of the Empire, but this was balanced by the

The colonnaded streets of Palmyra were evidence of the wealth derived by the city from its trading activities. (Ancient Art and Architecture)

substantial production of mines (such as the silver mines of Spain), imperial properties which were exploited under the protection of military units. In spite of the inflexibility of the tax system, imperial revenue tended to exceed expenditure during peace time, while wars could be supported, especially if they were of limited duration and generated some booty: the agricultural production of the provinces sustained both the imperial machine and the demands of local cities.

On the other hand, there were already ominous signs of strain in the second century, the golden age of imperial prosperity. The purity of the basic silver coin, the *denarius*, was reduced from about 90 per cent to 75 per cent, and then to 50 per cent under Septimius Severus. Prolonged warfare was expensive, especially along the European river frontiers where booty was unlikely to offset costs: troops had to be moved to the area of conflict, imposing demands on communities along their lines of march, and extra resources were demanded to make good losses. Civil war was an even worse prospect, partly because such conflicts were, at best, a zero-sum game (and at worst ruinously expensive to ravaged provinces and all who supported the losers), but more significantly because any attempt to secure the throne required lavish promises of donatives and higher pay for armies, which would also be expanded to meet the crisis. The plague brought back from the east by Lucius Verus' army in AD 167 was also a significant factor, and the consequences of the loss of agricultural population can be traced in papyrus records of land leases in Egypt: in some areas the impact seems to have lasted for a generation, in others three generations.

Cassius Dio, historian, twice consul and experienced provincial governor, writing about 230, assesses the change in the Empire's fortunes in 180 (72.36).

'[Marcus Aurelius] encountered a host of problems practically all through his reign ... he both survived himself and preserved the Empire in extraordinary and untoward circumstances. One thing alone marred his personal happiness: his son [Commodus] ... our history now falls away, as affairs did for the Romans of that time, from a realm of gold to one of iron and rust.'

The Empire functioned best when rulers survived for reasonably long reigns with the support of both senate and provincial armies, when conflicts remained localised and did not coincide with challenges on other frontiers, and when climatic and other conditions permitted a reasonable level of agricultural production. The accession of Septimius Severus in 193 provided a severe jolt, since this was followed by three years of internal conflict across much of the Empire. His son Caracalla, who succeeded in 211, had to buy favour with the troops by awarding a 50 per cent pay increase, financed by issuing a new (overvalued) silver coin and by doubling the 5 per cent inheritance tax: to increase the revenue from the latter, he gave Roman citizenship to all the free inhabitants of the Empire and so brought them into the tax net. The Empire survived Caracalla, but if the balance of imperial prosperity was delicate during the second century it now become precarious, with a major external threat or significant internal upheaval likely to generate a crisis.

Inside and outside the empire

Army of the Roman Empire

The Roman Empire depended on the power of its armies, which had always been composed of a combination of citizen and non-citizen troops. Before the universal extension of citizenship in AD 212 citizens were recruited into the legions, while non-citizens traditionally entered the auxiliary units. Remarkably little is known about the process of recruitment:

Late Roman cavalry. Artwork by Christa Hook. (Osprey Publishing)

Late Roman infantry. Artwork by Christa Hook. (Osprey Publishing)

conscription was probably always a feature, with manpower needs being apportioned in line with census records of citizens, but there was also some element of hereditary service as units drew on veteran settlements. At times, perhaps often, military service offered a reasonably good and quite safe career for the young provincials, especially if they served close to home.

In the later Empire it is often alleged that the balance of the armies changed, with citizens being outnumbered by foreigners, the traditional infantry backbone eclipsed by cavalry units, and frontier units (*limitanei*) relegated to an inferior status. Romans were progressively demilitarised and the increasingly un-Roman armies declined in discipline and loyalty. These theories reflect developments in the later army, although they are all ultimately misconceptions.

Roman armies did continue to rely on substantial units of non-citizens, especially when troops had to be recruited quickly, as in civil war and after military defeat, or for special expeditions. These 'outsiders' were often excellent troops who provided reliable bodyguards for emperors and generals, whose personal retinues of *bucellarii* (biscuit-men) might represent the elite part of an army. There were also several senior non-Roman commanders who played important political roles, especially during the fragmentation of the western Empire in the fifth century, but it is invalid to infer from their prominence that non-Romans also dominated the ranks of the army.

Infantry had always been the particular strength of the Romans, and it is true that cavalry units performed a more important role in late Roman armies, but there is little evidence to support the popular notion that the Romans switched to reliance on heavy-mailed cavalry, an anticipation of medieval knights. The Romans had a few units of mailed lancers (*clibanarii* or boiler-boys) in imitation of Parthian and Persian units, but mounted archers on the Hunnic model were probably more common. The sixth-century historian Procopius chose a horseman equipped with a composite bow to represent the ideal contemporary soldier. But infantry remained the basis for most armies, and Roman foot-soldiers, when properly trained and led, were capable of defying all opponents.

Another development in the late Roman army was that, from the fourth century, distinctions were drawn, in terms of status as well as rewards, between *limitanei* and troops of the *comitatus*, i.e. between more static provincial units and those which accompanied the emperor or senior generals. It is often claimed that *limitanei* became soldier-farmers, losing their military quality along with their professionalism, but that misrepresents the nature of the estates which helped to support them and ignores their continuing use in conjunction with mobile troops on major eastern campaigns. It is noticeable that the *limitanei* included more cavalry units than the *comitatus*, a reflection of the usefulness of horses for local patrolling and of the greater ability of infantry to retain fighting strength when required to move long distances quickly.

There had been a gradual change in the deployment of Roman armies. In the early empire legions were quartered in major bases near the frontier (e.g. Cologne), but military need dictated that units were detached for specific duties as frontier garrisons or in the interior. Later this ad hoc dispersal was consolidated so that troops were spread across provinces in numerous forts and cities. Emperors, however, also needed mobile forces for more rapid deployment. In the east there came to be two armies 'in the presence' stationed near Constantinople, and others in the Balkans and the east; in the west Gaul and Italy had their own armies until imperial authority contracted from the former.

Overall, Roman armies changed between the third and seventh centuries, but the majority of troops were drawn from the Empire's inhabitants. Specific upland regions had the reputation for producing good recruits: the Balkan highlands,

Late Roman parade helmet. (AKG London)

mountainous Isauria in southern Asia
Minor, and Armenia. Goths, Germans and
Huns also made important contributions,
but such soldiers often came from groups
who had been accepted into the Empire and
given lands with the explicit purpose of
providing recruits. To educated observers
from the cities, the people who wrote most
of our evidence, Roman armies undoubtedly
looked quite barbaric and undisciplined,
but the same could often have been said
about early imperial armies.

The size of late Roman armies is a complex
game for which most of the pieces are missing.
In the third century army units probably
numbered upwards of 350,000, with a further
40,000 in the navy. Numbers increased
significantly under Diocletian (284–305) and
Constantine (306–37), so that the total
military establishment exceeded 500,000 –

perhaps even 600,000. But paper strength will always have surpassed disposable strength, and many troops were committed to particular assignments so that only a small proportion of the total establishment could be deployed for individual campaigns. In the fourth century an army of 50,000 was large, and by the sixth century mobile armies rarely exceeded 30,000.

In spite of complaints about discipline, Roman training appears to have remained tough. A succession of military manuals indicates that attention was devoted to training and tactics, at least in the eastern

Folio from the *Notitia Dignitatum*, depicting the responsibilities of the Master of Offices which included the imperial weapons factories (*fabricae*). (MS Canon Misc. 378, f. 141r, Bodleian Library)

Empire, although it is probably correct that organisation, rather than basic military skill, increasingly emerged as the way in which Romans surpassed their opponents. The Romans had the capacity to co-ordinate troops over long distances to build up complex armies, with artillery units as well as infantry and cavalry, and then keep these supplied on campaign: the infrastructure of roads, warehouses, granaries, arms factories and the billeting arrangements generated a complex body of law, and enabled the Romans to move their men wherever they were needed.

Persian arrangements

Only in the East did the Romans face an enemy with a sophistication comparable to their own. The Iranian Sassanids supplanted the Parthian Arsacids during the 220s, imposing themselves as a new military elite on a heterogeneous population, which included substantial groups of Jews and Christians in densely populated lower Mesopotamia. Persian armies are not clearly understood, since almost all our knowledge comes from Roman informants reporting Persian actions during the repeated conflicts. One important strategic point to bear in mind is that, from the Persian perspective, their north-eastern frontier, the sector in which they confronted the nations of central Asia, took priority; we occasionally glimpse Persian action in this area, as when King Peroz led his armies to disaster against the Hephthalite Huns in the late fifth century, or during the service of the Armenian Smbat Bagratuni in the early seventh, but there is a substantial gap in our appreciation of Persian might.

The career of Smbat
The Armenian Smbat, a member of the noble Bagratid house, commanded cavalry for the Romans in the Balkans in the 580s, but was exiled to Africa for instigating revolt. In the 590s he reappears in Persian service, being appointed provincial governor by King Khusro II; he was trusted to suppress awkward rebellions in the east and received the nickname 'Joy of Khusro', but Khusro was reluctant to allow him to return to Armenia and Smbat was kept at court as an honoured advisor.

The Greek historian Theophylact preserves rare information on Persian military arrangements.(3.15.4)
  'For, unlike the Romans on campaign, Persians are not paid by the treasury, not even when assembled in their villages; the customary distributions from the king, which they administer to obtain income, are sufficient to support themselves until they invade a foreign land.'

Persian kings did not maintain a large standing army until at least the sixth century: there were garrisons in frontier cities and fortresses, but for major campaigns kings instructed their nobles to mobilise provincial levies. Minor gentry of free status served as mounted warriors providing a backbone, and they probably brought along their own retinues. The system was feudal, with royal land grants carrying an obligation to serve or send troops on demand; campaigns inside the Persian kingdom seem to have been unpaid, on the assumption that soldiers could support themselves from their estates, but payment was given for foreign expeditions. Feudal arrangements could be extended to attract troops from outside the kingdom – who worked for specific terms – but mercenaries were also recruited, sometimes from the Hunnic and Turkic tribes beyond the north-east frontier, sometimes from specific internal groups such as the Dailamites who inhabited the mountains south of the Caspian.

Persian armies are often associated with heavily mailed cavalry, but their most potent element were mounted archers: Roman tactical writers advised that the Persians could not withstand a frontal charge, but that any delay in engaging at close quarters would permit them to exploit their superiority at archery. The Persians were heirs to a long Middle-Eastern tradition of siege warfare and they had a formidable capacity to organise sieges, dig mines and deploy a variety of engines to capture even the most strongly fortified positions. In the sixth century there was a substantial overhaul of the tax system as well as a redistribution of land, which was intended to bolster royal power by permitting the payment of some permanent units, an imitation perhaps of the Roman *comitatus*. But the feudal link between king and nobility remained crucial, dictating that military prestige was essential for royal authority: kings might embark on foreign campaigns to acquire booty and prestige for internal consumption.

Enemies in Europe

The personal prestige of the war leader was also vital for Rome's various tribal enemies in Europe. These groups ranged from small war bands from an extended family or single village, through more complex clan and tribal bands into which the family units would be subsumed, to the occasional but mighty international federation. At the bottom of the scale were the Slav raiders who crossed the Danube in the sixth century; these might operate in groups of 200 or 300, perhaps accompanied by their families in wagons as they sought land for settlement.

Most of the German and Gothic groups who challenged the Empire were collections of such smaller clan or village units, united under the authority of a king. The right to lead depended ultimately on success, especially in warfare; although leading families (such as the Gothic Balti and Amali) attempted to create dynasties, these could not survive the shock of prolonged failure or the absence of a suitable war-leader. There was some instability in these groups, and units – such as the Carpi, who were prominent down to AD 300 – might disappear permanently; others such as the Lombards are absent from our sources for several generations before re-emerging in the sixth century. Such changes did not represent the elimination of these people but their subjection to a different elite which imposed its identity on its followers. Powerful German kings might be able to

mobilise 10,000 warriors, and larger forces – such as those that confronted Julian at Strasburg in AD 357 – could be produced through alliances. On rare occasions German leaders commanded larger numbers – the Amal-led Ostrogoths fielded 25,000–30,000 warriors after subsuming a rival Gothic group in the Balkans – but this was exceptional, the product of Roman power which forced tribes to coalesce or face defeat.

The most powerful Roman enemies were the supranational federations, represented by the Huns in the fifth century and the Avars in the sixth and seventh. These groupings swallowed the variety of smaller tribal units within their sphere of action, with terror and booty providing the cement; their existence required regular warfare, and their ruthless leaders had the manpower to overrun the defences of even major cities. Both Huns and Avars posed serious challenges to Roman authority, but their inherent instability was their undoing: Attila's death in 453 led to fatal dissension among his potential heirs, while the Avars never recovered from their failure at Constantinople in 626, since weakness at the top permitted constituent sub-groups to rebel. The image of the Huns is of nomadic warriors whose attachment to their horses was such that they could scarcely walk, and it is true that the various warrior elites will have fought as cavalry, but all these groupings could also field substantial infantry forces which would have been provided by less prestigious elements, for example the Slavs within the Avar federation.

Collectively Rome's enemies rivalled, or surpassed, its military strength, but the Romans could usually hold their own, partly through superior organisation and training, partly through strong defences, but above all by the strategy of trying to avoid simultaneous conflict on different frontiers. Along the Danube or Rhine tribal groupings might co-operate in the short term, but Roman diplomacy was adept at exploiting potential splits. Wider collaboration was extremely rare, the only real instance

Movement of Goths across Europe

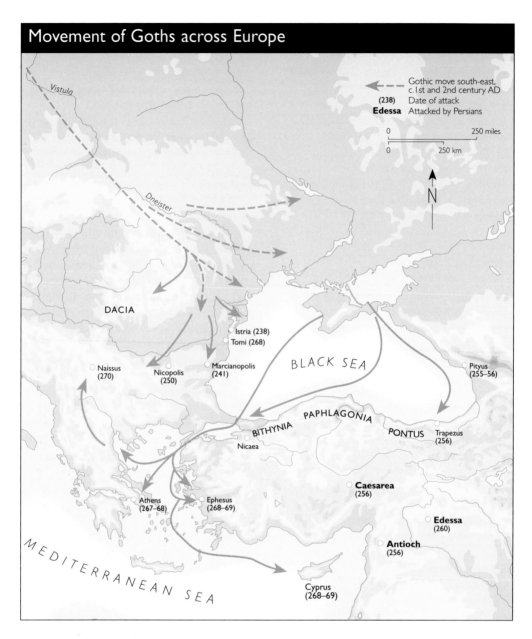

Gothic move south-east, c.1st and 2nd century AD

(238) Date of attack

Edessa Attacked by Persians

0   250 miles

0   250 km

N

Vistula

Dneister

DACIA

Istria (238)
Tomi (268)

Naissus (270)

Nicopolis (250)

Marcianopolis (241)

BLACK SEA

Pityus (255–56)

PAPHLAGONIA

BITHYNIA

PONTUS

Trapezus (256)

Nicaea

Caesarea (256)

Athens (267–68)

Ephesus (268–69)

Edessa (260)

Antioch (256)

MEDITERRANEAN SEA

Cyprus (268–69)

occurring in 626 when Persian troops encamped on the Bosporus attempted to join the Avar attacks on Constantinople, only to be thwarted by the Roman fleet. Possession of a small but powerful navy was a factor which distinguished the Romans from all their opponents, with the exception of Saxon raiders in the North Sea and the Vandal kingdom in North Africa which took over part of the western Roman fleet.

Creating crisis

After the murder of Severus Alexander in 235 the Roman Empire experienced 50 years of instability, commonly termed the Third-century Crisis, a period which marks the transition to the later Empire. The 'crisis' can be viewed from a number of interlocking aspects – frontier pressure, usurpers, religious change, financial shortages – but it is reasonable to begin from the frontiers: here developments can be identified which then arguably prevented the Empire from controlling change in other areas.

Beyond the eastern frontier a new dynasty was inaugurated when the Sassanid Ardashir was crowned in Ctesiphon in 226. The change was significant since the Romans had generally dominated the Parthians, and indeed repeated Roman successes had contributed to undermining royal prestige, but the Sassanids propagated a dynamic nationalism, including links with the Achaemenids, who ruled Persia before Alexander the Great's conquests. Embassies demanded the return of their ancestral property, with war as the consequence of the

The Greek historian Herodian records demands of a Persian embassy to Alexander Severus in the 220s (6.4.5).
'The mission declared that by order of the Great King the Romans and their ruler must abandon Syria and the whole of Asia opposite Europe, allowing Persian rule to extend as far as Ionia and Caria and the peoples within the Aegean-Pontus seaboard. For these were the traditional possessions of the Persians.'

inevitable refusal. Gordian's attempt to discipline Ardashir's son Shapur I ended in humiliation in 244, with Gordian defeated and murdered and his successor Philip the Arab forced to purchase the withdrawal of his army. Shapur's invasions in 253 and 260 resulted in the capture of Antioch, the major city of the eastern provinces as well as

The ruined walls of Dura by the River Euphrates. (Ancient Art and Architecture)

The Valerian Wall at Athens, cutting across the agora. (Author's collection)

numerous lesser places such as Dura on the Euphrates, and the transport to Persia of massive booty; Emperor Valerian was captured in battle at Edessa (Urfa) in 260 and taken back to Persia. For the next decade imperial authority in the east was limited, with the most effective resistance to the Persians being provided by the ruler of Palmyra, Odaenathus. The east had become an expensive military arena for the Romans, and the substantial tax revenues of its provinces were jeopardised.

The problem was compounded by events on the Danube, where the Romans also had to face a new enemy. Here change had been slow, the result of the gradual movement of Gothic peoples from northern Poland. The first attested Gothic incursion came in 238, when they sacked Istria near the Danube

mouth; a decade later they swept across the north-eastern Balkans, and Emperor Decius was killed and his army annihilated while trying to force them back across the Danube in 251. Further ravaging occupied the 250s, with the Goths commandeering shipping on the Black Sea to cross to Asia Minor and sail into the Aegean where they sacked Athens in 268. Mining operations in Macedonia and Thrace were inevitably disrupted.

This great movement of Goths naturally displaced other peoples who might find themselves squeezed against the Roman frontier; this process could trigger the formation of substantial federations as different tribes steeled themselves for the ultimate challenge of attacking the Romans. On the upper Danube the Vandals, Quadi and Marcomanni breached the frontier, and on the upper Rhine the Alamanni increased their strength to the extent that they twice invaded Italy in the 260s. On the lower Rhine

Porchester Castle. One of the late third-century Saxon shore fortifications, built to protect southern and eastern Britain from raids across the North Sea. (Ancient Art and Architecture)

the Franks gradually came to dominate another large federation which threatened frontier defences during the latter half of the century, and Saxon pirates began to raid across the North Sea and down the Channel.

Of the Roman world only Africa, the Iberian Peninsula and, to a lesser extent, Britain, were spared invasion. The cumulative nature of the frontier pressure is evident, with emperors unable to divert troops from one sector to another and instead constrained to confront invaders in conditions which led to defeat. The consequences for imperial prestige are obvious, and by the late 260s the Empire was virtually split into three units which attended separately to their own security. Trouble began in 235 when Severus

Alexander, who had just campaigned unsuccessfully in the east, was overthrown by the Rhine armies who feared his leadership. They proclaimed as their leader Maximinus the Thracian (allegedly an uneducated peasant risen from the ranks). Maximinus made no attempt to conciliate the senate, his control of the armies, especially those in the east, was shaky in spite of a promise to double military pay, and the extensive confiscations needed to provide funds for his promises damaged his reputation further. Maximinus survived until 238 when his failure to deal with rivals supported or proclaimed by the senate caused his troops to mutiny. Seven emperors within one year, fighting in North Africa and northern Italy, and disturbances in Rome were a foretaste of the anarchy to come; such substantial internal upheavals naturally afforded external enemies a chance to invade, which then increased the problems for whoever happened to occupy the throne.

The rapid turnover of emperors is best illustrated by a simple list – with the proviso that it is difficult to include all the shorter-lived local claimants to the throne.

235–38	Maximinus
238	Gordian I & Gordian II
238	Balbinus & Maximus
238	Pupienus
238–44	Gordian III
244–49	Philip the Arab
249–51	Decius
251–53	Trebonianus Gallus
251–53	Volusianus
253	Aemilianus
253–60	Valerian
253–68	Gallienus
268–70	Claudius II Gothicus
270	Quintillus
270–75	Aurelian
275–76	Tacitus
276	Florianus
276–82	Probus
282–83	Carus
283–85	Carinus
283–84	Numerian

Each new emperor meant another donation to the troops; each bout of civil war more loss of life, physical destruction and distraction from the frontiers. Ironically, in 248 Philip celebrated the millennium of Rome's foundation in spectacular fashion, but the military reverses of the 250s effectively split the Empire into three. Odaenathus' defence of the east fuelled ambitions for imperial authority, which were inherited by his wife Zenobia in 268/9, while in Gaul, the Rhine armies proclaimed their successful general Postumus. The air of crisis generated apocalyptic literature in the east (for example, the *Thirteenth Sibylline Oracle*), and a circuit of walls for Rome, 11.8 miles (19 km) in length, was rapidly constructed in 271. The Empire was only reunited by Aurelian in a series of energetic campaigns, which were helped by instability in Gaul following the murder of Postumus in 269 and by the death of Odaenathus; also, he was prepared to abandon the exposed province of Dacia and redeploy Roman troops along the lower Danube. Perhaps most significantly, the energetic Shapur died in 270 and it was to be 50 years before the Persians had a comparable leader. If military failure guaranteed overthrow, success did not ensure survival: both Aurelian and Probus, who continued Aurelian's re-establishment of the Empire, succumbed to plots in military camps, and Carus died while invading lower Mesopotamia, allegedly struck by lightning.

Aurelian's wall at Rome. (Ancient Art and Architecture)

Prolonged warfare inside the frontiers, regular defeat, and the rapid turnover of emperors cumulatively had major economic consequences. Emperors required more money to pay donatives and salaries to their troops, and the available supplies of bullion had to be squeezed in order to produce the necessary precious metal coins. Under Gallienus this resulted in the silver content of the *denarius*, the standard coin for military pay, declining to 5 per cent; subsequently there were issues of bronze washed in arsenic to provide a short-lived silvery brightness. The declining value of coinage triggered an offsetting rise in prices which resulted in an inflationary spiral, particularly during the last third of the third century.

One victim of inflation was the government, whose tax revenues declined in value; granted the inflexibility of the tax system, it was difficult to raise large new sums of cash. A consequence was an increasing reliance on taxation in kind: troops needed to be supplied and, rather than extracting increasingly worthless coin from rural taxpayers to permit units to purchase food and other necessities, the cycle was short-circuited by the transfer of goods directly to the troops. This development might have been accidental and haphazard, with armies gradually adopting the practice of securing their own supplies and leaving provincial administrations to acknowledge that their appropriations could be offset against tax demands. Other victims of inflation were the cities, where the spectacular building developments of the previous 150 years ceased.

Gold medallion of Valerian I and Gallienus Salonim proclaiming Concordia Augustorum. (© R Sheridan Ancient Art and Architecture)

Coin with legend *Carausius et fratres*, c. AD 286.
(Ancient Art and Architecture)

Another consequence of crisis was the
marginalisation of the senate and a
professionalisation of military command. In
238 the senate and armies had contested the
imperial succession, but under Gallienus
senators were effectively removed from
military commands. This development
had begun earlier, since the Severans
had sometimes preferred trustworthy
non-senators for important commands, but
the insecurity of emperors furthered the
change while troops also demanded reliable
leaders rather than aristocratic amateurs.
When Aurelian came to power with the
backing of the upper Danube legions and
then used these troops to restore the

Empire, it transpired that Pannonians, and
other officers of Balkan extraction, became
prominent. These were professional soldiers,
at whom civilian intellectuals might sneer
for their lack of culture, but they proved
to be solidly committed to the idea of
Rome and its traditions, as well as
effective generals.

The crisis also had a religious impact, since
a natural inference from repeated misfortune
was that the gods had to be placated. At first
this took the form of intensified supplication
to traditional deities: in 249 Decius issued a
general instruction to all citizens to offer
prayers and sacrifices on his behalf. A
consequence, probably unintended, of this
order was that Christians were faced with the
choice of disobedience or apostasy; some
abandoned the faith, many more probably

Radiate coin of Aurelius (AD 270–275). (Barber Institute of Fine Arts)

found means to evade or connive in the ruling, but there were enough martyrs to identify Christians as traitors to the Empire. Persecution lapsed with Decius' death, but was restarted in 257 by Valerian who specifically targeted the Christians, with attention focused on the priestly hierarchy; his defeat in battle terminated proceedings. The successful Aurelian advertised his devotion to the traditional divinities, especially Victoria, Mars, Hercules and Jupiter who were all connected with success in war, and to these he added a special devotion to the cult of the Unconquered Sun, *Sol Invictus*, after the defeat of Palmyra in 273. Devotion to the correct divinity did bring success, as Diocletian and Constantine would continue to demonstrate in their different ways.

A papyrus of AD 250 demonstrates the consequences of Decius' demand for sacrifice: everyone needed a receipt to prove compliance.

'To those superintending the sacrifices of the village of Theadelphia, from Aurelia Bellias, daughter of Peteres, and her daughter Capinis. We have sacrificed to the gods all along, and now in your presence according to orders I have poured a libation and offered sacrifice and eaten of the sacrificial offering; we ask you to sign below to this. Farewell.

Signatures: We Aurelius Serenus and Aurelius Hermas saw you sacrificing. Signed by me, Hermas.

Year 1 of the Emperor Caesar Gaius Messius Quintus Traianus Decius Pius Felix Augustus, Payni 27.'

Challenges to empire

Diocletian's stabilisation

Aurelian reunified the Roman Empire, but Diocletian re-established imperial stability through a reign of 20 years which ended in planned retirement. The secret of success was an imperial college, since one factor promoting earlier disunity had been the desire of major armies to have their own emperor. Power-sharing had worked in the second century when Marcus Aurelius co-opted Lucius Verus to command his Parthian campaign, and was tried in the third century by the families of Valerian and Carus. Family control might enhance loyalty, but perhaps at the expense of ability. Diocletian elevated a long-standing colleague, Maximian, to the rank of Caesar in 285 and dispatched him to Gaul to quell an uprising of *bacaudae*, rebels who have been variously interpreted as Robin Hood-style brigands or supporters of local warlords. In 286 Maximian was promoted to Augustus, with the relationship between the Augusti represented by their divine companions, Jupiter king of the gods

An orator in Gaul addresses Maximian in 289, praising his co-operation with Dioecletia (Latin Panegyrics 10.11).
   'Your harmony has this result, invincible princes, that even Fortune responds to you with an equally great measure of success. For you rule the State with one mind, nor does the great distance which separates you hinder you from governing, so to speak, with right hands clasped. Thus, although your doubled divinity increases your royal majesty, by your unanimity you retain the advantage of an undivided Empire.'

for Diocletian and Hercules his son for Maximian. After six years of joint reign, rebellion in Egypt prompted Diocletian to increase his imperial resources by appointing two junior colleagues as Caesars, Galerius for the east and Constantius for the west. Marriage between the Caesars and daughters of the Augusti united the Tetrarchy.

   The energetic campaigning of Diocletian and his colleagues is reflected in the victory titles which precede his Edict on Maximum Prices of 301:
   'The emperor Caesar Gaius Aurelius Valerius Diocletianus, pious, fortunate, unconquered, Augustus, pontifex maximus, Germanicus maximus six times, Sarmaticus maximus four times, Persicus maximus two times, Britannicus maximus, Carpicus maximus, Armenicus maximus'.

   Constantius was sent to recover Britain, which permitted Maximian to leave the Rhine frontier and move to Africa to deal with Moorish incursions. In the east the major achievement was Galerius' success against the Persians in 298, after initial defeat in the previous year. The decisive action was Galerius' capture of King Narses' womenfolk, although he also ravaged lower Mesopotamia. Narses sued for peace and surrendered territory east of the Tigris to recover his women.

   Almost as important as the victories was Diocletian's administrative overhaul, which doubled the number of provinces – where governors were expected to keep closer control of their areas – and introduced dioceses which grouped provinces and provided a judicial buffer between the governor and the praetorian prefect at court. The tax system was reformed perhaps to distribute the burdens of land and poll tax more fairly, perhaps to improve efficiency. Provision was made for regular reassessment; for the first time it was theoretically possible to construct an imperial budget. Diocletian also attempted to stabilise the coinage, with new issues of gold, silver and bronze, but he seems to have lacked the bullion to issue enough precious metal coins to convince people. As a result inflation continued, and in 301 Diocletian issued an Edict on Prices, a law for display in all towns and markets of the Empire on which was listed the maximum prices for a wide range of goods and services. In terms of military organisation, Diocletian may have been less innovative than in other areas, although the evidence for his actions is indecisive. His concern for frontiers was reflected in the strengthening of defensive installations, the construction of new roads – for example the Strata Diocletiana which ran from the Gulf of Aqaba to the Euphrates – and the deployment of troops near the frontiers. The army most probably increased in size during his reign, though there are no precise figures.

Diocletian explains the need to control prices. (Preamble to Edict on Maximum Prices.)

'Who does not know that wherever communal safety requires our armies to be sent, profiteers insolently and covertly attack the public welfare, not only in villages and towns, but on every road? They charge extortionate prices for merchandise, not just fourfold or eightfold, but so that human speech cannot find words to characterise their profit and practices. Indeed, sometimes in a single transaction a soldier is stripped of his donative and pay. Moreover, the contributions of the whole world for the support of armies fall as profits into the hands of these plunderers, and our soldiers appear to bestow with their own hands the rewards of military service and their veterans' bonuses upon the profiteers.'

Constantine and conversion

Diocletian retired in 305, to a specially prepared palace at Spalato (Split), but his succession arrangements faltered because they disregarded the soldiers' strong dynastic loyalties: when Constantius the new

Towers at Constantina (modern Viransehir, Turkey). The large horseshoe towers of basalt date back to the fourth century. (Author's collection)

Augustus of the west died at York in 306, his troops promptly acclaimed his son Constantine. Over the next six years Constantine schemed and fought his way to mastery of the whole western Empire, a process which culminated outside Rome at the battle of the Milvian Bridge in 312: his opponent, Maxentius, son of Diocletian's partner Maximian, deployed his troops on the north bank of the Tiber, but they were routed and during the confused flight back to the city the wooden bridge collapsed. The

most significant aspect of the victory was that Constantine's men fought under the sign of Christ, whose inspiration Constantine proclaimed; after the battle he set about rewarding his new God. In some ways this marked a decisive change from Diocletian (who had initiated persecution of Christians in 303) and Constantine's conversion did eventually lead to the Christianisation of the Empire and so of Europe, but the underlying religious attitude was the same: correct worship of the right divinity provided victory.

A contemporary Christian teacher, Lactantius, records how Constantine had the chi-rho monogram (the first two Greek letters of Christ's name) painted on his soldiers' shields (On the Deaths of the Persecutors 44.5–6).

'Constantine was advised in a dream to mark the heavenly sign of God on the shields of his soldiers and then engage in battle. He did as he was commanded and by means of a slanted letter X with the top of its head bent round, he marked Christ on their shields. Armed with this sign, the army took up its weapons.'

For the next 12 years Constantine shared the Empire in uneasy partnership with Licinius in the east, but in 324 the two clashed in a decisive naval engagement in the Bosporus, with Constantine emerging as sole ruler of the whole Empire. This victory was marked by the construction of a new capital – Constantinople – on the site of the old city of Byzantium, which gained new walls, a palace and the other appurtenances of an imperial seat. Constantine now inherited responsibility for the Danube and Persian frontiers. During the 330s he campaigned energetically against the Goths, to such effect that the area was quiet for the next generation. Towards the end of his reign tension began to rise in the east, with Constantine probably contacting the

Constantine writes to the king of Persia (Eusebius, Life of Constantine 4.9–13).

'With God's power as ally I began from Ocean's shores and progressively raised up the whole world with sure hopes of salvation ... I believe that I am not mistaken, my brother, in confessing this one God the Author and Father of all, whom many of those who reigned here, seduced by mad errors, have attempted to deny. But such punishment finally engulfed them that all men saw that their fate superseded all other examples, warning those who attempt the same ends ... With these persons – I mean of course the Christians, my whole concern is for them – how pleasing it is for me to learn that the chief regions of Persia too are richly endowed! ... These therefore I entrust to you, since you are so great, putting their persons in your hands, because you too are renowned for piety.'

Christian population of lower Mesopotamia to raise hopes of 'liberation'; he had already written to the young Persian king Shapur II to inform him of the benefits of Christianity and to warn him not to harm his Christian subjects. In the event Constantine bequeathed the conflict to his successors, since he died near Nicomedia in 337 at the start of the march east.

Although his accession disrupted the Tetrarchy, Constantine was in most ways a true heir to Diocletian's purpose. For half his reign Constantine was involved in civil conflicts, which diverted attention from frontiers: he reorganised the central forces which accompanied the emperor, the *comitatus*, and created two prestigious commands for cavalry and infantry, the *magister equitum* and *magister peditum*. The praetorian prefect lost operational military responsibility, but took overall charge of administration, including military supplies and recruitment; in recognition of this increased role, the Empire was divided into four grand prefectures. At provincial level military command was also separated from civilian duties. Constantine's greatest achievement was the establishment of a stable currency, based on gold *solidi* struck at 72 to the pound: the bullion gained from civil war and confiscations of temple treasures underpinned this coinage.

The eastern Empire

The Empire was divided between Constantine's three surviving sons, Constantine II in Gaul, Constans in Rome, with Constantius II in the east inheriting the war against Shapur. Constantius II has suffered historiographically, since most Christian writers regarded him as heretical, while the major contemporary secular author, Ammianus Marcellinus, misrepresented him because of his clash with the pagan Julian. As a result his dogged conduct of 24 years of war with Persia is underrated, although he managed to preserve the eastern frontier with only limited losses in the face of one of the most dynamic Persian rulers. There was only one pitched battle during the conflict, outside Singara in 344: the Romans had the advantage until a disorderly pursuit and attack on the Persian camp permitted the enemy to recover so that the engagement ended indecisively. Constantius' strategy was to build new forts and rely on the major cities of the frontier to hold up Persian incursions, with Nisibis holding the key to advances across upper Mesopotamia: Shapur besieged the city three times, bringing the full might of Persian siege technology to bear, but the defences held, with divine support provided through the city's deceased bishop, Jacob, whose corpse was paraded around the ramparts as a talisman. Singara, however, was captured in 360 when a newly repaired section of wall was undermined, and Bezabde also fell that year.

The siege of Amida (Diyarbakir) in 359, of which Ammianus was a fortunate survivor, illustrates the dynamics of strategic confrontation. Constantius was engaged on the Danube, when Shapur II planned to strike deep into Roman territory, for once disregarding Nisibis. The Romans implemented a scorched-earth policy and placed strong guards at the Euphrates crossings, but the river was in flood and the Persians turned northwards. At Amida Shapur attempted to overawe the defenders by a display of might, but a Roman artilleryman disrupted proceedings when a bolt aimed at the king struck a member of his entourage. Shapur felt obliged to punish the city, which eventually fell after 73 days of determined resistance, but the combination of delay and heavy casualties terminated the Persian invasion.

Civil conflicts as well as the demands of other frontiers distracted Constantius, especially after he became sole ruler in 353. Between 351 and 353 Constantius co-opted his cousin Gallus to supervise the east, but he proved unsuitable. In 355 Constantius turned to Gallus' younger brother, the intellectual Julian, and used him to control the west, with better results until in 360 Julian's troops – quite possibly with Julian's encouragement – demanded imperial equality for their commander. Constantius stabilised the frontier before turning west to confront his rival, but he died en route; Julian inherited the Empire without a battle.

Julian arrived in the empire of the east in 361 with a reputation as a successful general and a need to demonstrate that he could surpass Constantius. A major factor in this was religion: Julian espoused the old gods and had renounced formal adherence to Christianity when challenging Constantius. Persia offered the great testing ground, where Julian could prove the rectitude of his beliefs and the pusillanimity of Constantius' policies. Preparations were made for a grand invasion in 363: Julian himself would lead an army down the Euphrates while a second army created a diversion in northern Mesopotamia. The campaign began well, with Julian overrunning Persian forts along the Euphrates and reaching the vicinity of the capital Ctesiphon in spite of Persian

The arch of Galerius, Thessaloniki, showing fighting between Romans and Persians. (Author's collection)

attempts to thwart his advance by breaching their irrigation canals. However, he now realised that he had little chance of capturing the city, and resolved to march back up the Tigris; this entailed burning his fleet of supply ships which could not be hauled upstream. Treacherous guides led him astray and then Shapur, whose army had not been tied down effectively in the north, began to harass; Julian was mortally wounded in a skirmish, and his successor, the officer Jovian, could only extricate his army by surrendering territories to the east of the Tigris, plus

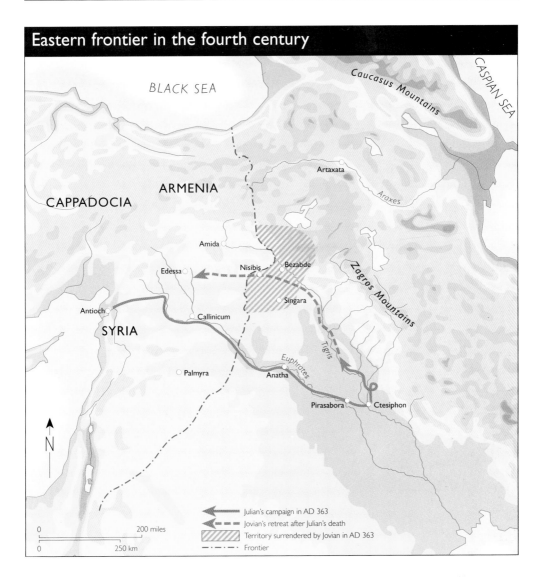

Eastern frontier in the fourth century

BLACK SEA

Caucasus Mountains

CASPIAN SEA

Artaxata

ARMENIA

CAPPADOCIA

Araxes

Amida

Zagros Mountains

Edessa   Nisibis   Bezabde

Singara

Antioch

Callinicum

SYRIA

Tigris

Palmyra   *Euphrates*   Anatha

Pirasabora   Ctesiphon

N

←───	Julian's campaign in AD 363
◀----	Jovian's retreat after Julian's death
▨	Territory surrendered by Jovian in AD 363
─·─·─·	Frontier

0 ———— 200 miles

0 ———— 250 km

Nisibis and Singara. Bitter opposition from the inhabitants of Nisibis who pleaded to continue their battle with the Persians was overruled, and they were resettled in Amida.

Blame for the Roman reverse was allocated in accordance with religious loyalties: for pagans the heroic Julian's success was squandered by the cowardly Jovian, whereas for Christians Jovian's piety rescued the Romans from Julian's folly. The loss of Nisibis rankled, and its recovery was still on the imperial agenda two centuries later, but the agreement of 363 ushered in the most prolonged period of peace which the Roman eastern frontier had ever

experienced, a fact crucial for the eastern Empire's survival during the fifth century. There were moments of tension, and two brief conflicts, but no prolonged warfare until 502. Tension persisted for a time, primarily over control of Armenia, but this was settled in 387 when the Armenian kingdom was suppressed and its territory partitioned between Rome and Persia. In 421/2 war was provoked by the behaviour of Christian activists in Persia against Zoroastrian shrines; the Christians fled west and Theodosius II refused to surrender his co-believers. In 440–42 conflict flared again, this time over Roman payments for the

The Baptistery at Nisibis with the lintels of the original doors just visible. Only a year after the building's dedication Nisibis was transferred to Persian control by Jovian (AD 363). (Author's collection)

defence of the Caucasus; the Romans once more had the better of limited fighting. On each occasion the Romans were prompted to agree peace because of Hunnic activity in the Balkans, while the Persians also had distractions on their north-eastern frontier.

During these years there emerged a system of diplomatic arrangements, which reduced the risks of disagreements spilling over into full-scale war. The rights of minority religions were recognised, which protected the Christians in Persia; their position also became easier when doctrinal questions separated them from Roman Christians. Attempts were made to regulate the transhumant Arab tribes of the frontier, construction of new fortresses was banned, the defence of key fortifications in the Caucasus was accepted as a shared burden, and trade was funnelled through specific markets at Nisibis, Callinicum and Artaxata. Rome and Persia came to see themselves as the two lights of the world, with a mutual obligation to help each other against disruptive and uncivilised outsiders. There was even a story that Emperor Arcadius appointed his Persian counterpart Yazdgard as guardian for his infant son Theodosius.

Khusro appeals to Emperor Maurice,
recalling the tradition of collaboration
between their states. (Theophylact 4.11.2–3)
'God effected that the whole world
should be illumined from the very
beginning by two eyes, namely by the
most powerful kingdom of the Romans
and the most prudent sceptre of the
Persian state. For by these powers the
disobedient and bellicose tribes are
winnowed and man's course is
continually regulated and guided.'

European frontiers in the fourth century

After Constantine's death, the crucial factor
in the west was civil war: Constantine II was
killed while fighting Constans in 340; in 350
Constans was overthrown by Magnentius, an
officer on his personal staff, who then
dispatched a rival in Rome. Constantius, after
seducing the troops of another usurper in
Illyria, clashed with Magnentius at Mursa on
28 September 351 in one of the most
destructive battles of the century. Once
Magnentius was eliminated after a further
defeat in 353, the Rhine armies were again
disrupted when court intrigues pushed a
Frankish general Silvanus into revolt in 354;
finally Julian (who had been sent to Gaul in
355 because internal conflict had permitted
Franks and Alamanni to breach the frontier)
was acclaimed Augustus at Paris in February
360; he marched his best troops east to
confront Constantius.

Julian's actions in Gaul are painted in rosy
colours by Ammianus, whose surviving books
open with the suppression of Silvanus, a
daring action in which Ammianus
participated. During 356 Julian campaigned
energetically and re-established Roman
authority along the Rhine. In 357 an
ambitious campaign was planned to take the
war into Alamannic territory, with the armies
of Gaul and Italy operating a pincer
movement. Problems of co-ordination

(perhaps compounded by jealousies)
unravelled the strategy and the army of Italy
was defeated near Basel. But in August Julian
confronted the Alamanni on the right bank
of the Rhine near Argentoratum (Strasburg): it
was a hard-fought struggle. Since Ammianus
described it in reasonable detail, it is one of
the few battles in late antiquity whose course
can be reconstructed. Ammianus commented
that superior Roman discipline and training
overcame the Alamanni's advantage in
physical size, which gave their intitial charge
such ferocity; it is also noticeable that the
battle was won by the Roman infantry,
whereas their cavalry, which included some
heavy-armed cataphracts (suit of armour), was
forced to flee.

After Jovian's brief reign, the brothers
Valentinian and Valens shared the Empire,
with the senior Valentinian taking charge of
the Rhine and upper Danube and Valens
responsible for the lower Danube and east.
On the Danube the stability established by
Constantine was broken, the reason, as so
often, Roman internal conflict. The Goths'
relations with Constantius had moments of
tension, especially when imperially
sponsored attempts to promote Christianity
provoked a backlash, but they remained
allies of the house of Constantine to the
extent that when Procopius, Julian's cousin
(and hence distant relative of Constantine)
revolted against Valens in 365, he was able
to secure help from the Tervingi, the main
confederation on the Danube. Thereafter
Valens set about disciplining these rebels, but
severe flooding and the Goths' ability to
disappear into the swamps and mountains
prevented a decisive encounter. When Valens
halted proceedings in 369, the Tervingi
secured better terms, which included a
reduction in their obligation to provide
troops for the Romans. South of the river
Valens embarked on energetic fortification,
while the Tervingi returned to persecution of
Christians. Further west Valentinian was
engaged in similar operations against the
Alamanni, Quadi and Sarmatians, while his
subordinates dealt with disturbances in
North Africa and Britain.

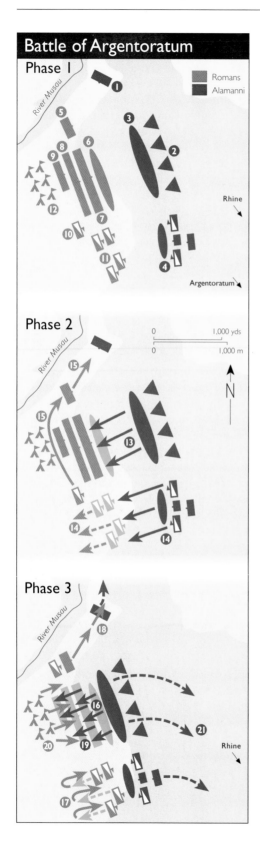

Battle of Argentoratum

Phase 1

Romans
Alamanni

River Musau

Rhine

Argentoratum

Phase 2

River Musau

0   1,000 yds
0   1,000 m

N

Rhine

Phase 3

River Musau

Rhine

LEFT BATTLE OF ARGENTORATUM

Phase 1: 1 Alamanni infantry in ambush; **2** Main Alamanni infantry in wedge formation; **3** Alamanni skirmishes; **4** Alamanni cavalry; **5** Roman flank guard under Severus; **6** Roman light infantry; **7** Roman front line including Cornuti and Brachiati; **8** Roman second line including Batavi and Reges; **9** Roman reserve including Primni; **10** Julian's personal guards; **11** Roman cavalry; **12** Roman baggage and camp guards.

Phase 2: 13 Alamanni infantry drives Roman light infantry behind front line; **14** Alamanni cavalry routs Roman cavalry on right wing; **15** Alamanni ambush discovered and neutralised by Roman left wing, helped by Julian's personal guard.

Phase 3: 16 Alamanni break through Roman front line, but are held by second line; **17** Julian re-forms Roman cavalry and stabilises right wing; **18** Roman left wing pursues Alamanni ambush from field; **19** Alamanni drive back Roman lines to foot of hill where camp sited; **20** Roman reserve and camp guards push Alamanni back; **21** Alamanni flee towards Rhine, pursued by Romans.

RIGHT BATTLE OF ADRIANOPLE

Phase 1: Roman army deploys from front line of march with cavalry on the right wing and light infantry in lead. **1** Gothic wagon circle defended by infantry; **2** Gothic light infantry; **3** Roman light infantry; **4** Roman cavalry on right wing (*sagitatti* and *scutarii*); **5** Roman heavy infantry; **6** Roman cavalry on left wing; **7** Roman reserves (Batavi); **8** Gothic cavalry (arriving late).

Phase 2: While Goths try to delay the battle to allow their cavalry to return, the two armies come to blows. **9** Gothic infantry withdraws to laager during negotiations; **10** Sagitatti and scutarii repulsed; **11** Main Roman infantry force attacks laager; **12** Part of cavalry on Roman left wing attacks laager; **13** Gothic cavalry returns, shatters Roman left wing; **14** Roman cavalry on left still forming up.

Phase 3: 15 Most Roman cavalry driven from field; **16** Roman reserves withdraw; **17** Roman army trapped between Goths counterattacking from laager and Gothic cavalry.

In the 370s the position on the frontiers changed. In the west Valentinian suffered a stroke while trying to overawe a delegation of Quadi, and was succeeded by Gratian, whose military experience was limited, and the infant Valentinian II. On the lower Danube masses of Goths arrived to pester Roman officials for the right to cross and settle peacefully. Their desperation was caused by the westward movement of the Huns, who had been displaced from further east and were now approaching the Black Sea with a

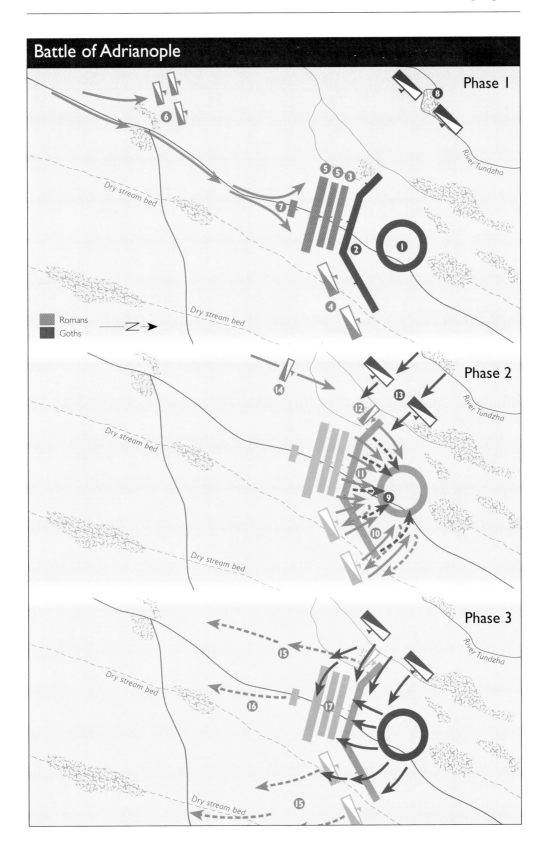

Battle of Adrianople

Phase 1

Phase 2

Phase 3

Romans
Goths

consequent domino effect on the tribes there. The most powerful Gothic group, the Greuthungi, who had been based between the Dneister and Dneiper, was destroyed and the Tervingi were the next to be threatened: the might of Rome appeared less daunting than the Hunnic scourge, and the Danube seemed to offer safety. Roman attempts to control the Goths, by admitting only the Tervingi and removing their leaders failed, but thereafter they managed to contain the Gothic threat quite successfully by exploiting control of food and by harassing the Goths as soon as they dispersed to seek supplies.

In 378 it appeared that the Romans would crush the Goths as Valens returned from Antioch and Gratian marched from the Rhine to co-operate against them. However, Gratian's arrival was delayed when the Alamanni heard about his plans and decided to invade. Valens still felt confident of defeating the Goths, and on 9 August 378 he led his army out of camp at Adrianople towards the Gothic position. The Romans probably outnumbered the Goths, but their deployment from the line of march was confused and the battle was joined haphazardly, with the result that the Roman wings were driven back. At this moment the Gothic cavalry, which had been absent foraging, returned and the combination of their flank attacks, the heavy fire of Gothic archers, and the heat of the long day gradually wore down the Roman centre. Resistance was stubborn, but two-thirds of the army, including Valens, were killed.

Adrianople is often seen as the turning point for the Roman Empire, but it is necessary to remember that the eastern forces survived the destruction of one of its field armies and the Gothic victors were successfully managed by the new eastern Emperor, Theodosius, who gave them lands in Thrace in return for military service. They were a major nuisance, but their inability to capture walled cities limited their impact. Gothic help was fully exploited when Theodosius was drawn westwards to

intervene against usurpers, first in 387 and then in 394: the destruction of these battles, especially at the Frigidus River in 394, certainly weakened the Goths, but more importantly they destroyed the best elements in the western armies. When Theodosius died at Milan in AD 395 the Empire was divided between his young sons, Arcadius in the east and Honorius in Italy. It was the east which was in a much stronger position, as can be seen from the increasingly desperate legislation on recruitment and other military matters issued by Honorius' court over the next dozen or so years.

Ammianus reports the recognition by the victor of Adrianople that his men could not attack cities (31.6.4).

'Fritigern realised that it was pointless for men without experience of siege-works to fight at such a disadvantage. He suggested that the siege should be abandoned and a sufficient force left behind to contain the enemy. He had no quarrel, he said, with stone walls, and he advised them to attack and pillage in perfect safety rich and fruitful regions which were still unguarded.'

Ammianus (16.2.12) made the same point with regard to the Alamanni. 'They avoided the actual towns as if they were tombs surrounded by nets.'

The Huns

The Huns began to arrive along the Danube in the early fifth century, but until AD 395 their epicentre had been further east as they had raided across the Caucasus. In 408/9 a Hunnic chief Uldin crossed the lower Danube but his followers were seduced by Roman diplomacy. By the middle of the next decade the Huns were established on the Hungarian plains, and their approach should probably be connected with the construction of a

Defences at Diocletianopolis (modern Hissar, Bulgaria) showing the characteristic late Roman brick-banded rubble core of city walls. (Author's collection)

The Greek historian Priscus, who served on an embassy to Attila's court, records Hunnic demands. (fr.11)

'Edeco came to court and handed over Attila's letters, in which he blamed the Romans in respect of the fugitives. In retaliation he threatened to resort to war if the Romans did not surrender them and cease cultivating the territory he had won, extending along the Danube from Pannonia to Novae in Thrace; furthermore, the market in Illyria was not to be by the Danube as previously, but at Naissus, which he had laid waste and established as the border between Scythian and Roman territory, it being five days' journey from the Danube for an unladen man. He ordered that ambassadors come to him, not just ordinary men but the highest ranking of the consulars.'

massive new set of walls for Constantinople in 413.

In the 420s Hunnic power expanded through subordination of neighbouring tribal groups and consolidation of authority within a single ruling family, that of Rua, who was succeeded by his nephews, Attila and Bleda. Rua extracted annual peace payments from the eastern Empire, which were 700 pounds of gold in the 430s increasing to 2,100 pounds in 447 (perhaps 5 per cent of total imperial revenue) at the height of Attila's power. During the 440s Attila ravaged the northern Balkans, sacking cities and driving off booty to fuel Hunnic prosperity, but in 450 he turned westwards where Honoria, sister of Emperor Valentinian III, offered herself in marriage.

Hunnic raids and disintegration of the west

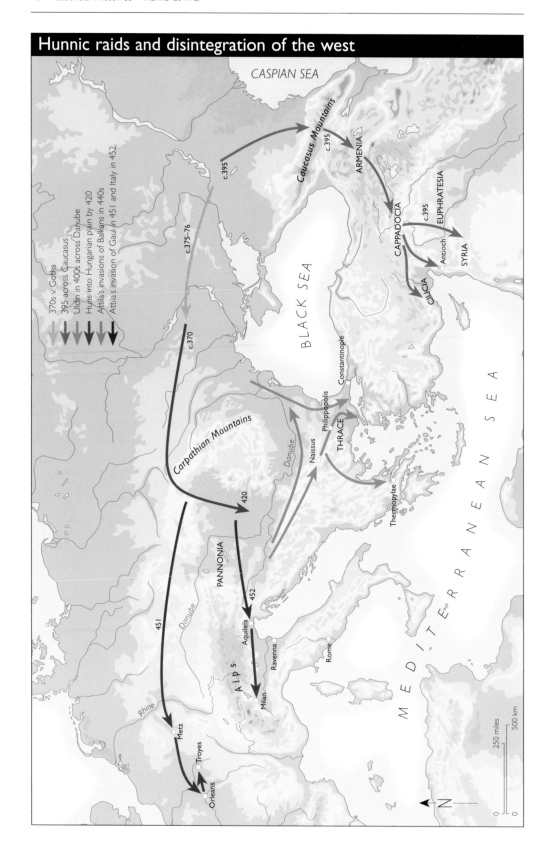

CASPIAN SEA

CAUCASUS Mountains

c.395

c.395

ARMENIA

EUPHRATESIA

c.395

CAPPADOCIA

Antioch

CILICIA

SYRIA

BLACK SEA

c.375-76

c.370

Constantinople

Philippopolis

THRACE

Naissus

Danube

Carpathian Mountains

Thermopylae

420

PANNONIA

452

Danube

MEDITERRANEAN SEA

451

Aquileia

Ravenna

Rome

Alps

Rhine

Milan

Metz

Troyes

Orleans

370s v. Goths
395 across Caucasus
Uldin in 400s across Danube
Huns into Hungarian plain by 420
Attila's invasions of Balkans in 440s
Attila's invasion of Gaul in 451 and Italy in 452.

N

250 miles

500 km

Hunnic power depended upon the personal authority of their leader, his ability to dominate all members of his federation. This was achieved partly through the exercise of patronage and the disbursement of the rewards of military victory, but even more by the exercise of sheer terror: Attila repeatedly demonstrated that it was impossible to escape his grasp, and potential rivals were painfully killed. As a result the Romans could not operate their traditional diplomatic strategy of divide and subvert: they were required to hand back Huns, who were probably refugees from Attila's power, and so were denied the chance to cultivate alternative leaders. Attila was also a skilled diplomat, with a wide knowledge of the international scene: he knew the invasion routes into Persia, timed his attacks on the Balkans to coincide with an eastern military expedition to Africa, and exploited tensions between Goths, Franks and Romans in the west; his reception of Roman envoys was a masterful demonstration of psychological pressure. As his federation expanded he came to control vast military resources, which it was in his interest to exploit. His armies, spearheaded by Hunnic cavalry, were capable of rapid movement to anticipate defences, while the masses of expendable subordinates could be thrown at Roman walls to supplement the Huns' considerable skill at siegecraft. The threat was such that Constantinople was provided with a further set of fortifications, the Long Walls, which stretched from the Sea of Marmara to the Black Sea.

Salvation for the Romans lay in the fact that the Hunnic federation could not stand still: military success and booty were regular requirements, and any interruption created tensions within the international conglomeration. Attila's attacks on the west produced only limited success, and this jolt was compounded by his death: his sons fought over the succession, and subordinate tribes rebelled: in 454 the Gepids and then the future Ostrogoths, Lombards, Heruls plus others emerged from the shadow of Hunnic control to confront the Romans along the Danube frontier. For the next generation the northern and central Balkans were repeatedly crossed by Gothic groups in search of land and safety, while the Romans reverted to reliance on fortifications and control of food supplies, plus the incentive of imperial military titles with their accompanying salaries, to hold the balance. The Goths recognised the Roman strategy of playing off different groups, and on occasions tried to counteract this, but the incompatible ambitions of Gothic leaders played into Roman hands. Only the opportune death of one powerful leader permitted his main rival Theoderic the Amal to unite most of the Balkan Goths into an army whose strength was such that the Emperor Zeno commissioned them to invade Italy and reassert imperial control there.

Two Gothic leaders (Theoderic Strabo – son of Triarius – and Theoderic the Amal) reproach each other for playing into Roman hands. (Malchus, fr. 18.2.30–38)
    'But the son of Triarius kept riding up to the other's camp, insulting and reproaching him and calling him a swearer of useless oaths, a child and a madman, an enemy and betrayer of his own race, who did not know the Romans' mind or recognise their intentions. "For they remain at peace, while the Goths wear each other down. Whichever of us loses, they will be the winners without effort."'

Loss of the west

In 395 the young Honorius succeeded Theodosius, but the west was controlled by Stilicho, a general of Vandal descent. Stilicho claimed that the dying Theodosius had also instructed him to protect the eastern emperor Arcadius, and that two Balkan provinces should be transferred to western authority. This rivalry drew Stilicho into Balkan affairs, where imperial competition permitted the Goths (who had been weakened by casualties

Ivory plaque depicting Stilicho as defender of the state.
(Ancient Art and Architecture)

in Theodosius' service) to demand a better
deal. Alaric, a Gothic commander under
Theodosius, emerged as leader of a force
capable of withstanding an imperial army, but
he still struggled to secure lasting benefits:
success only came after other tribal groups
breached the western frontiers.

On 31 December, 406 Vandals, Alans and
Sueves swarmed across the Rhine, triggering
the proclamation of local commanders as
emperors. Stilicho's authority crumbled, and
his family – which had been trying to marry
into the imperial house – was eliminated;
with it disappeared the main Roman army in
northern Italy, since many of Stilicho's
Gothic troops chose to join Alaric. Alaric
failed to obtain concessions from Honorius

(who had abandoned Milan for the greater
security of Ravenna), established his own
emperor, and on 24 August 410 captured
Rome.

This brief sack of Rome was of symbolic
significance; of greater importance were
Honorius' imperial rivals in Gaul and Spain
whose ambitions permitted the invading
tribes to exploit Roman divisions. Honorius
had already demonstrated his inability to
protect his subjects in his desperate military
legislation of the previous decade. Inevitably
local protectors appeared who had to exploit
the available military manpower, which was
often roaming tribal bands: incompatible
objectives emerged, with the policy of
crushing invaders at odds with a desire to
preserve their manpower for future use.

Alaric died while trying to reach Africa,
and his followers, whom it is now convenient
to call Visigoths (west Goths), moved to
Spain where they helped to subdue the
Sueves and Vandals. In 418 they eventually
settled in the Garonne valley in south-west
Gaul, where Honorius granted them estates
with their revenues; in return they were to
campaign for Honorius, who sent them back
to Spain. Theoderic (417–51) gave essential
stability: he challenged the Romans in
southern Gaul whenever they seemed weak,
and expanded his power in Spain by building
links with the Sueves, while appearing
co-operative when it suited his interests.

One consequence of Visigothic
involvement in Spain was the Vandal crossing

to Africa, although the precise cause was, naturally, internal Roman conflict: Boniface, governor of Africa, invited the Vandals to help him to resist pressure from rivals at Ravenna. The Vandals' arrival in 429 condemned the western Empire: within a decade they had taken over the north African provinces, captured Carthage (in 439) and withstood eastern empire attempts to repulse them. North Africa was the most prosperous part of the west, and its wealth had escaped the impact of tribal invasion; its loss decisively reduced the resources on which emperors at Ravenna could call and, to compound the problem, the Vandals used Roman ships at Carthage to dominate Sicily and Sardinia and to ravage Italy; they sacked Rome in 455, a much more destructive event than Alaric's entry in 410.

From the Roman perspective the priorities were to restore battered imperial authority, stabilise the tribal groups, and then gradually weaken their independence. In the latter part of his reign Honorius relied on the general Constantius, who was granted the title of patrician, which thereafter became the designation for the senior western commander. Constantius married Honorius'

daughter (Galla Placidia – the widow of Athaulf), but died in 421. At Honorius' death in 423, Constantius' widow appealed to Constantinople on behalf of her infant son, Valentinian while a usurper at Ravenna sought help from the Huns. Valentinian III was installed in 425, but the dispute brought the Huns into western empire affairs.

Aetius emerged as the new patrician. His greatest achievements were in Gaul, where he contained the Visigoths – often with help from the Huns whom he also used to crush the Burgundians. Aetius had been a hostage with the Huns and so was well connected, but the culmination of his successes was the repulse of Attila's invasion in 451 at the battle of the Catalaunian plains, with the help of an improbable coalition of Franks, Burgundians and Visigoths (whose king Theoderic died heroically). When Attila turned to northern Italy in 452, Aetius could not prevent the loss of northern cities including Aquileia. He could harass the Huns but without bringing the Visigoths across the Alps he dared not attack directly – instead

The Gallic chronicler Hydatius describes the loss of Spain (Chronicle, 17).

'When the province of Spain had been laid waste by the destructive progress of disasters just described, the Lord in his compassion turned the barbarians to the establishment of peace. They then apportioned to themselves by lot areas of the provinces for settlements: the Vandals took possession of Gallaecia and the Sueves that part of Gallaecia which is situated on the very western edge of the Ocean. The Alans were allotted the provinces of Lusitania and Carthaginiensis, and the Siling Vandals Baetica. The Spaniards in the cities and forts who survived the disasters surrendered themselves to servitude under the barbarians, who held sway throughout the provinces.'

The King of the Visigoths marries a captured imperial princess in 414 in a ceremony intended to signal a rapprochement between Romans and Goths (Olympiodorus, 24).

'Athaulf married Placidia at the beginning of January in the city of Narbo at the house of Ingenuus, one of the leading locals. There Placidia, dressed in royal raiment, sat in a hall decorated in Roman fashion, and Athaulf sat by her side, wearing a Roman general's cloak and other Roman clothing. Amidst the celebrations, along with other wedding gifts Athaulf gave Placidia 50 handsome young men dressed in silk clothes ... Then nuptial hymns were sung, first by Attalus, then by Rusticius and Phoebadius. Then the ceremonies were completed amidst rejoicings and celebrations by both the barbarians and the Romans amongst them.'

Disintegration of the west

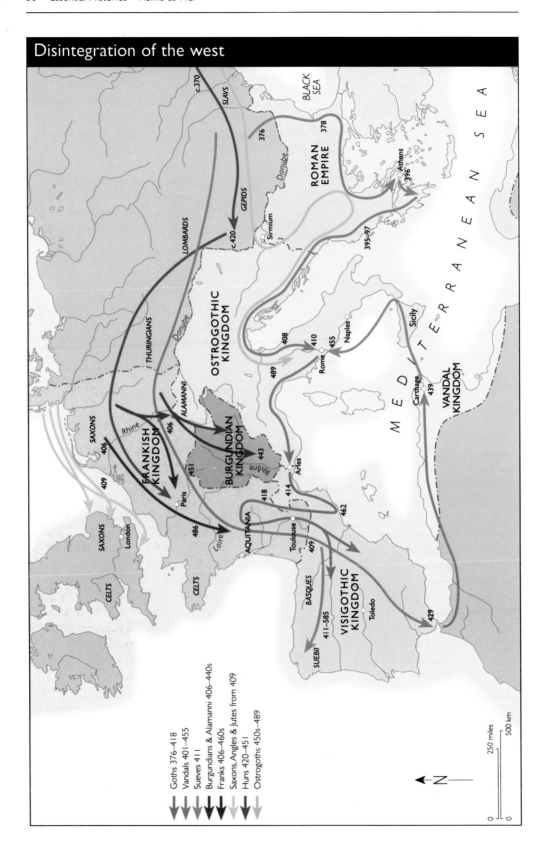

Goths 376–418
Vandals 401–455
Sueves 411
Burgundians & Alamanni 406–440s
Franks 406–460s
Saxons, Angles & Jutes from 409
Huns 420–451
Ostrogoths 450s–489

Pope Leo was deployed to encourage Attila to leave.

Mosaic in S. Apollinare Nuovo, Ravenna, depicting the palace of Theoderic. (Ancient Art and Architecture)

Like Stilicho and Constantius before him, Aetius schemed to link his family to the emperor by marriage, but this contributed to his downfall. In September 454 Valentinian personally assassinated Aetius, only for Aetius' bodyguards to take revenge in March 455. For the next two decades control was contested between the different power blocks with interests in the western state: the Visigoths, Vandals, the eastern Empire and the Italian army under the patrician Ricimer, backed a rapid succession of rulers. The problems are illustrated by the reign of Majorian (457–61), Ricimer's appointee, who curbed Vandal raiding in central Italy and reasserted Roman authority in Gaul and Spain; he appears to have been too successful for when an attack on Africa was foiled, Ricimer had him executed.

One final attempt to crush the Vandals and restore western resources was made in 468 when a massive naval expedition was

An appreciative assessment by a Latin author of Theoderic the Ostrogoth's regime in Italy (Anonymus Valesianus 59–60).

'Theoderic was a man of great distinction and of good-will towards all men, and he ruled for 33 years. Italy for 30 years enjoyed such good fortune that his successors inherited peace, for whatever he did was good. He so governed two races, Romans and Goths, that although he was an Arian, he nevertheless did not attack the Catholic religion; he gave games in the circus and amphitheatre, so that even by Romans he was called Trajan or Valentinian, whose times he took as a model; and by the Goths, because of his edict in which he established justice, he was judged in all respects to be their best king.'

sent from Constantinople, but this was thwarted by Vandal fireships. Failure was ruinous for the eastern state – which spent 64,000 pounds of gold (more than a year's revenue) – and fatal for the western state: in 476, after a rapid turnover of rulers, the army of Italy under Odoacer deposed the young Romulus, who was derisively nicknamed Augustulus ('little Augustus'), and returned the imperial insignia to Constantinople. Odoacer controlled Italy until Theoderic the Amal took Ravenna in 491 and established the 'Ostrogothic' (east Goth) kingdom. Theoderic in his long reign (491–526) created a successful Romano-Gothic realm during which Italy prospered and a ruler at Ravenna secured considerable power in southern Gaul and Spain and intermittent influence in Vandal Africa.

Sixth-century wars

While the western Empire floundered towards disintegration, the eastern Empire prospered, in spite of repeated destruction in the Balkans, since the eastern frontier was quiet and the rich provinces of Asia Minor, Syria and Egypt generated surpluses. Eastern rulers attempted to help the west, especially in the struggle against the Vandals, whose maritime raiding threatened to affect the eastern Mediterranean, but to no avail. Conflict resumed with Persia in 502 when King Kavadh invaded Armenia, capturing

various fortresses and finally, after a fierce siege, Amida. The origins of the outbreak lay much further east in Persian dealings with the Hephthalites of central Asia, who had helped Kavadh regain his throne; they were now demanding subsidies and Kavadh asked the Romans for financial help but the eastern emperor Anastasius refused, perhaps reviving the issue of Persian control of Nisibis or perhaps just reluctant to build up Persian strength.

The Roman response was slow since Bulgar Huns were ravaging the Balkans in 502, but the position slowly stabilised, in spite of dissension between Roman commanders; by 505 Kavadh was distracted by another Hephthalite invasion and agreed a truce for seven years. Anastasius interrogated his generals about their problems, and the lack of a secure base near the frontier was identified as a key. Therefore a site was chosen at Dara and construction of a massive new fortress was undertaken; financial responsibility was entrusted to Bishop Thomas of Amida. By 507 he had raised the walls to a sufficient height to disregard Persian protests that the Romans had breached the agreement to ban new frontier fortifications.

In spite of this tension the truce persisted for a further 20 years, although competition

The southern watergate at Dara showing the full height of the wall (the upper half has now fallen), part of a tower and the arches of a bridge over the stream. (The Bell Collection, University of Newcastle.)

The southern watergate at Dara, from inside the city, showing the two stages of the construction of the circuit wall. The first stage, 30 feet (10 m) high, was constructed by Anastasius, while the thinner arcaded superstructure is Justinianic. (The Bell Collection, University of Newcastle.)

between the two superpowers of the ancient world continued on the fringes of their spheres of influence, in sub-Caucasia and Arabia where religious factors exacerbated tensions. But the occasion for renewed conflict in 527 came from an incident which reflected the continuing strength of the fifth-century traditions of peaceful co-operation: the elderly Kavadh asked Emperor Justin to adopt his son Khusro and so guarantee his succession in a mirror image of Arcadius' appeal to Yazdgard over a century before; Justin was persuaded that full adoption might compromise the Roman succession and so offered Khusro a lesser form of adoption.

The war began badly for the Romans with reverses in Armenia and upper Mesopotamia, but Justinian, who succeeded his uncle in autumn 527, reorganised eastern defences by creating a new military command for Armenia, initiating major defensive works at key sites, and appointed a new general for the eastern command, Belisarius. (Procopius, the main historian for Justinian's wars, joined Belisarius' staff). In 530 the Persians were defeated in Armenia and Belisarius overcame the Persian army outside his base of Dara, but these victories were offset in 531 when Belisarius was defeated at Callinicum on the Euphrates. Justinian's main concern

An example of the international links constructed by Theoderic, who here writes to the Burgundian king to accompany the gift of a clock and urge the benefits of 'civilisation'. (Cassiodorus, Variae *1.46)*

'Therefore I greet you with my usual friendship, and have decided to send you by the bearers of this letter the time-pieces with their operators, to give pleasure to your intelligence ... Possess in your native country what you once saw in Rome. It is proper that your friendship should enjoy my gifts, since it is also joined to me by ties of kinship. Under your rule let Burgundy learn to scrutinise devices of highest ingenuity and to praise the inventions of the ancients. Through you it lays aside its tribal way of life and, in its regard for the wisdom of its king, it properly covets the achievements of the sages.'

Eastern campaigns in the sixth century and Heraclius' campaigns against the Persians

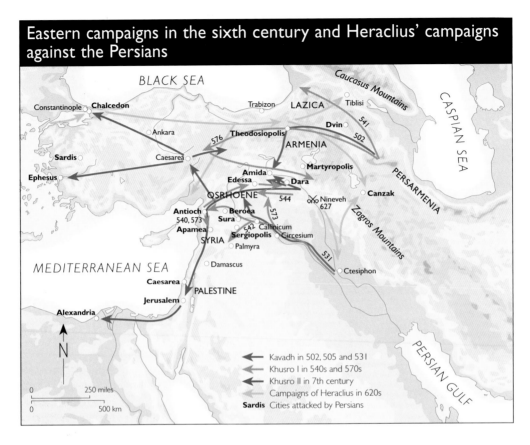

throughout had been to stabilise the situation on the eastern frontier, and negotiations were now pursued to achieve the Endless Peace to which the new Persian king Khusro agreed in 532: Justinian paid 11,000 pounds of gold, and agreed to withdraw the Roman commander and his troops from Dara.

From the start of his uncle's reign in 518 Justinian had been interested in western affairs and had rapidly rebuilt links between the Eastern Church and the Pope at Rome. This caused strain in Ostrogothic Italy where the Goths, in spite of their heretical status, had sustained good relations with the papacy because of tensions between Rome and Constantinople. The death of Theoderic the Amal in 526 and the struggle of his daughter Amalasuintha to retain the throne for her son Athalaric upset the international balances which had developed in the west during the previous generation. Peace with Persia provided Justinian with the opportunity to advance his grand idea.

The Vandals came first: they were the more obnoxious to eastern Christians because some mutilated refugees from their intermittent persecutions had reached Constantinople. There had been two eastern expeditions against them during the fifth century, and the prospects for diplomacy were better in Ostrogothic Italy. In 533 an expedition sailed in 500 transports escorted by 92 warships and comprised 15,000 Roman soldiers, 1,000 foreign allies and Belisarius' retainers, his *bucellarii*. The Vandal king, Gelimer, was distracted by rebellion on Sardinia whereas Belisarius received help with supplies from the Ostrogoths in Sicily, and the Romans landed without encountering the Vandal fleet. Belisarius advanced on Carthage, defeated a scratch army raised by Gelimer, and captured the city; later that year, when their troops had returned from Sardinia, the Vandals attempted to recapture Carthage but they were heavily defeated just outside the walls.

Justinianic defences at Martyropolis (modern Silvan, Turkey) built when the city became the base for the new general of Armenia. (Author's collection)

Justinian reorganised the province, restoring urban fortifications which the Vandals had slighted, reconstituted frontier defences, and returned property to the Catholic Church. Belisarius sailed to Constantinople with several thousand Vandal captives, who were enrolled in the eastern armies, and was permitted to celebrate a triumph, the first non-imperial triumph for over 500 years.

An opportunity now presented itself in Italy where Athalaric had died and Amalasuintha, imprisoned by her cousin Theodahad, was killed. Justinian protested, and sent expeditions to Dalmatia and Sicily. Negotiations with Theodahad about accepting Roman suzerainty broke down, and Belisarius was ordered to invade Italy, even though he had been sent to Sicily with only 7,000 Roman soldiers, 500 allies and his *bucellarii*: he captured Naples by siege – although some inhabitants supported the Goths – and then marched into Rome from which the garrison had withdrawn. Theodahad had now been replaced by

Vitigis, who moved to besiege Rome in February 537; in spite of shortages of troops and supplies Belisarius defended the massive circuit, and gradually harried the besiegers so that they were suffering as much as the defenders when the siege was ended in winter 537/8. The arrival of reinforcements permitted Belisarius to take the offensive and he secured Liguria, Milan and Rimini, but disagreements between Roman commanders, especially those involving Narses, who did not recognise Belisarius' seniority, led to disaster when an invading army of Burgundians sacked Milan; allegedly 300,000 of its male inhabitants were massacred. Narses was recalled to Constantinople, and in 539 Belisarius drove the Goths out of all Italy south of the Po valley and began to close on Ravenna, whose surrender was negotiated in 540.

So far the reconquest had been a spectacular success since with limited forces the eastern Romans had eliminated two powerful western kingdoms, in spite of the distraction of regular incursions into the Balkans by Bulgars and Slavs, and of problems with mutinies and raiding Moors in Africa. The key was peace in the east, but

The walls at Edessa (Urfa, Turkey) which withstood three Persian sieges during the sixth century. (Author's collection)

in 539 this was breaking down at the time Khusro, perhaps already jealous of Justinian's western victories, received an embassy from Vitigis urging him to act before Justinian became too powerful. A quarrel over grazing rights between allied Arabs gave Khusro an excuse to attack, and in 540 he marched up the Euphrates to seek booty or protection money: cities on his route were stormed or intimidated into buying protection, and Antioch was captured after a fierce siege; it was systematically ransacked to the extent that marbles and mosaics were transported to Persia, while the surviving inhabitants were marched off to found a city of New Antioch near Ctesiphon. During his return to Persia more cities were pillaged or coerced into buying safety. Khusro's successes are often cited as proof that Justinian neglected military matters, but the truth is that, although Roman defences were in a reasonable state, scattered garrisons had no chance of opposing a Persian royal army; there was little to be done except to hold out

in defended cities until mobile units were sent from Constantinople.

In 541 Khusro switched his attention to Lazica in the north, while Belisarius, who had been recalled from Italy to handle the situation, raided into upper Mesopotamia. In 542 Khusro intended to move on Palestine, but was dissuaded by improvements in Belisarius' army. Another factor may have been bubonic plague, which was raging in the Roman Empire. In 543 plague halted Persian moves in the north, but in 544 Khusro returned to Mesopotamia with the specific target of Edessa. Religion appears to have been the main cause, because Edessa was believed to have received a guarantee of protection from Christ in the form of a letter which was engraved over the city gates. Khusro therefore deployed all the resources of Persian siege technology, only to be thwarted, and the story emerged that his great siege mound had been destroyed through the intervention of a miraculous icon of Christ – the start of the fame of the Mandylion of Edessa, the future Shroud of Turin. In 545 Khusro agreed a truce for five years, in return for 5,000 pounds of gold and the provision that operations could continue

The Greek historian Menander records the ratification of peace with Persia in 561/2 (fr.6.1.304–19).

'When these and other matters had been thoroughly debated, the 50-year treaty was recorded in Persian and in Greek, and the Greek was translated into Persian speech and the Persian into Greek. Those of the Romans who ratified the concordats were Peter the Master of Offices and Eusebius and others, while of the Persians Yazdgusnasp the Zikh and Surenas and others. When each side's agreements had been entered in the records they were compared to establish the identity of their contents and wording.

The first clause was written that through the pass at the place called Tzon and the Caspian Gates the Persians should not admit either Huns or Alans or other barbarians to gain access to the Roman realm, and that the Romans should not in that region or in other parts of the Median frontier send an army against the Persians.'

in Lazica; the truce was extended in 551 and again in 557 before a peace agreement for 50 years was signed in 561/2. The treaty contained very detailed provisions about frontier relations, as well as a guarantee from Khusro that he would not persecute his Christian subjects.

In Italy the Roman position soon deteriorated. The Goths believed that Belisarius had tricked them into surrender by appearing to agree to become their ruler and so, although they had lost Ravenna, they chose a new leader. Totila proved to be a dynamic commander: Roman forces initially outnumbered him, but these were dispersed and their individual commanders failed to co-ordinate their actions. As a result Totila recovered much of southern Italy in 542 and starved Naples into submission in 543. Belisarius returned in

Mosaic of Justinian accompanied by Bishop Maximian, civilian dignitaries and bodyguards. From S. Vitale, Ravenna. (Ancient Art and Architecture)

544 to confront the crisis, with 4,000 new recruits but little money, but he was unable to engage the Goths. Totila captured Rome in 546 and, though Belisarius recaptured it the next year, his lack of resources led him to request a recall. When Totila regained Rome in 550 and threatened Sicily, Justinian was eventually prompted to act. Narses was sent to end the war, having demanded the resources which he deemed necessary. In 552 and 553 he twice defeated the Goths; he then had to deal with a horde of Franks and Alamanni who had taken the opportunity to invade Italy, but in 554 peninsular Italy was firmly under Roman control and at peace. Narses was left in charge of the reorganisation of the country with combined civilian and military authority.

One criticism of Justinian's grand reconquest is that it overstretched east Roman resources, so that his successors struggled to cope with the various challenges of the late sixth century. If hindsight makes this apparent, the contemporary perspective needs to be remembered: Justinian pacified the east to the best of his ability before embarking on his western ambitions and, even though Khusro broke the peace agreement, the frontier was again stabilised after the losses of 540; bubonic plague exacerbated Roman problems, but the prosperity of Africa in the late sixth century illustrates that peace could have brought long-term dividends.

Fortifications at Dara showing main horseshoe towers and smaller intermediate square towers. The citadel is visible in the middle distance. (Author's collection)

Invasion of the Balkans in the sixth century

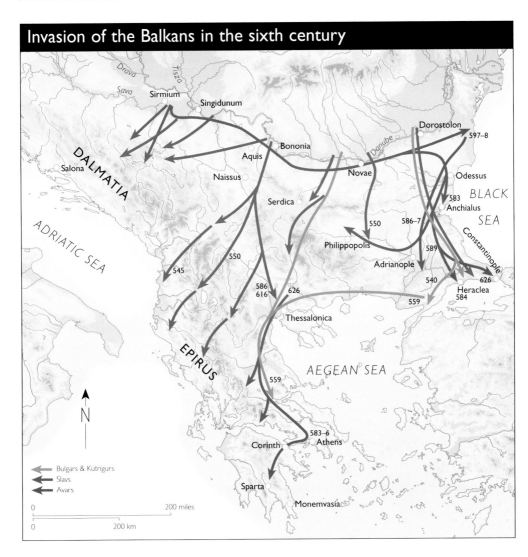

Justinian's successors

Unfortunately a new threat emerged in the late 550s, when Avar envoys contacted the Roman commander in the Caucasus. Like the Huns, the Avars were the former elite of a central Asian federation who had been forced to flee westwards, and they shared the Huns' grand ambitions and ruthless purpose. Once they occupied the Hungarian plain the Balkans, a military backwater under Justinian, became a serious problem again; the threat of Avar domination prompted the Lombards to migrate to Italy where they overran Roman positions in the Po valley. Justin II, who had succeeded his uncle in 565, had grand ideas

about Roman dignity: he dismissed Avar requests for subsidies and then provoked war with Persia. His bellicose behaviour was not complete folly, since he believed that the Turks in central Asia would co-operate by attacking the Persians on their north-eastern frontier, and a revolt of the Christian aristocracy of Persian Armenia suggested that Khusro had further distractions: Justin asserted that he could not abandon his co-believers and refused to make the annual payments agreed under the 50-year peace.

Justin's ambitions were not matched by action and in 573 the Persians captured Dara after a six-month siege: the shock sent Justin mad, and the Romans were compelled to seek a truce. In 576 Khusro campaigned into Armenia, but failed to take any cities and was outmanoeuvred in the mountains; the royal baggage was captured and many Persians were drowned when escaping across the Euphrates. Thereafter the Romans generally contained Persian attacks while ravaging their territories so that Khusro and his successor Hormizd (578–90) were prompted to pursue negotiations. These, however, foundered on the Roman insistence on recovering Dara and peace was only restored in 591: Hormizd was overthrown following disagreements with his leading general Vahram, and his son Khusro II fled to the Romans when Vahram approached Ctesiphon to beg for help. The Romans restored him to power, in return for concessions in the sub-Caucasian principalities and the restoration of Dara and other places captured in the war.

Eastern campaigns traditionally took precedence over other theatres for the Romans, and during the 570s and 580s the Balkans and Italy were neglected: the main impediment to Lombard progress were their own disputes, while in the Balkans Tiberius had few troops with which to repel the Avars when they turned their attentions south in 579. For the next decade the Romans had to rely on increased peace payments and urban defences, which the Avars – like the Huns before – captured. In the early 580s Slav bands pushed south – partly in conjunction with the Avars and partly to escape their domination – ravaging Athens and Corinth, approaching the Long Walls of Constantinople in 584, and attacking Thessalonica in 586.

Maurice, who succeeded Tiberius in 582, could do little until the eastern peace permitted him to transfer troops. Thereafter he embarked on an energetic series of campaigns which gradually stabilised the Danube frontier from the Delta to Singidunum (Belgrade) and permitted the Romans to reassert their authority in the interior. The war was carried north of the river, first in attacks on the Slavs across the lower Danube and then into the Avar

homeland on the Hungarian plains. But constant fighting gradually took its toll, and in 602 the army, already discontented over changes to military pay (which reduced the cost of equipment and horses) mutinied when it was ordered to stay north of the Danube for winter campaigning. A march on Constantinople toppled Maurice and installed the officer Phocas in his place.

Phocas' accession would inevitably have reduced the intensity of Roman activity in the Balkans, but it had more serious consequences: Khusro II seized the excuse provided by the overthrow of his protector, Maurice, to attack the Romans in order to recover the possessions and prestige he had lost in 591. During Phocas' reign (602–10) the Persians gradually captured the Roman positions east of the Euphrates, often after prolonged sieges. In 609/10 Heraclius, the son of the governor of Africa, revolted against Phocas, whose regime in Constantinople had become increasingly unpopular and violent; the distraction of civil war once more proved the Romans' undoing. Heraclius captured Constantinople in 610, but was not fully in control of the east until 611/12, by which time the Persians had pushed on to Antioch and Caesarea (Kayseri) in Cappadocia.

Heraclius was no more successful than Phocas in stemming their advance: in 614 Jerusalem fell to a Persian siege, its inhabitants and the relics of Christ's passion being taken into Babylonian captivity; Egypt was invaded in 616 and captured completely in 619, depriving Constantinople of its food supply and the Empire of its richest province. In 622 Heraclius in desperation 'borrowed' the wealth of the Constantinopolitan Church and embarked on a series of campaigns which assumed the aspect of a crusade: Khusro II, who had flirted with conversion to Christianity in 590/1, now showed himself to be an intelligent enemy of the orthodox, since he favoured the Jews and tolerated heretical and dissident Christian groups. At least Heraclius could legitimately present himself as defender of the faith. Heraclius abandoned attempts to defend Roman territory and instead took the war into Persia, basing himself in Armenia and the sub-Caucasian principalities, ravaging Azerbaijan, and avoiding the Persian armies which attempted to trap him.

War in the east had again led to neglect of the Balkans, and in the first quarter of the seventh century Slavs and Avars took control of much of the north and the centre. Heraclius had no troops to oppose their advance, and he had come close to capture himself in 623 when organising a diplomatic reception for the Avar Chagan near the Sea of Marmara: apparently Heraclius was forced to scamper back to Constantinople with his crown under his arm. Escalating peace payments were the only solution, but these did not work in the face of growing Roman weakness. In 626 the Avars besieged Thessalonica and then turned their attention to Constantinople, which was subjected to fierce bombardment by massed siege engines and waves of Slav attackers. A Persian army encamped on the Bosporus liaised with the Chagan, and an attempt was made to ferry Persian soldiers to reinforce the assault, but their crossing was disrupted by the Roman navy. Roman ships were also instrumental in breaking up a Slav attack across the Golden Horn, and the Avar Chagan was forced to withdraw with his prestige badly dented; stories soon emerged about the divine protection which the Virgin Mary gave the city which housed several of her relics.

Heraclius had declined to return to protect his capital, and his decision to focus on the eastern war was justified. First, with the assistance of Turkish allies he ravaged Persian territory extensively and then, after the Turks withdrew beyond the Caucasus, he defeated the Persians in battle outside Nineveh in December 627. The threat to

This message from Heraclius announcing the overthrow of Khusro II was read out in the Church of S. Sophia at Constantinople (Chronicon Pashale p.728).

'Let all the earth raise a cry to God; serve the Lord in gladness, enter into his presence in exultation, and recognise that God is Lord indeed. It is he who has made us and not we ourselves. We are his people and sheep of his pasture.

And let all we Christians, praising and glorifying, give thanks to the one God, rejoicing with great joy in his holy name. For fallen is the arrogant Chosroes, opponent of God. He is fallen and cast down to the depths of the earth, and his memory is utterly exterminated from earth; he who was exalted and spoke injustice in arrogance and contempt against our Lord Jesus Christ the true God and his undefiled Mother, our blessed Lady, Mother of God and ever-Virgin Mary, perished is the profaner with a resounding noise.'

central Persia led to a palace coup against Khusro, with his son agreeing to peace with Heraclius in return for support. This ushered in a period of extreme instability at the Persian court with a succession of short-lived rulers, including a Christian general in Khusro's service. From this chaos Heraclius extracted the return of Roman territories and the spoils taken from Jerusalem, including the relic of the Holy Cross, which Heraclius reinstalled in its rightful place in a grand ceremony at Easter 630. The Roman world appeared to have been put to rights and a period of consolidation and recovery could begin.

Brothers in arms

Abbinaeus, commander of provincial garrison

Flavius Abbinaeus joined the army in 304/5 and served for 33 years in the contingent of 'Parthian Archers' based in middle Egypt; this was a mounted unit whose name indicates that it was originally raised for service on the eastern frontier, or from captives taken on that frontier, but which was later recruited in the normal way from Roman provincials. In 337/8 Abbinaeus, now a non-commissioned officer, escorted an embassy of Blemmyes (tribesmen from the southern Egyptian border) to Constantinople, where he was promoted to protector by Constantius, a step which included the honour of being allowed to kiss the purple imperial robe. Protectors operated as a group of junior staff officers who undertook a variety of imperial business, and Abbinaeus was detailed to escort the embassy home; after three years among the Blemmyes, Abbinaeus returned to Constantius, who was then in Syria, and received promotion to command the cavalry squadron at Dionysias.

Back in Egypt Abbinaeus faced competition for this position since others also had secured letters of appointment through patronage. Abbinaeus appealed to Constantius and had his post confirmed, but in 344 he was dismissed by the local Count; his position was ratified on appeal. He then remained in office until after 351. The desirability of Abbinaeus' command is revealed by a collection of papyri which illustrate the vicissitudes of his career, the interaction of his troops with the local population, and his soldiers' close involvement in the maintenance of law and order and the extraction of imperial revenues from their district.

Alaric, Roman officer and tribal warlord

Alaric was born in about 370 into the Balthi, a leading family among the Gothic Tervingi. As a youth he probably participated in the Danube crossing of 376 and observed the subsequent encounters with imperial forces; at some stage he became an Arian Christian, the standard creed among the Goths. By the early 390s he had emerged as leader of a warband in the Balkans who opposed Emperor Theodosius, but in 394 he commanded tribal allies in Theodosius' expedition against the western usurper Eugenius. Disenchanted by inadequate recompense for his contribution to victory at the Frigidus River and the heavy casualties suffered by his followers, he proceeded to ravage the central and southern Balkans, taking advantage of tensions between Rome and Constantinople. By 399 he had secured one major wish, the senior Roman command of General of Illyricum, which provided him with salaries and provisions for his followers.

In 401 he invaded Italy and besieged the western emperor Honorius in Milan, but was defeated by the western generalissimo Stilicho; he was forced to withdraw to the Balkans as his men suffered from heat and poor food. He remained in the north-eastern Balkans, attempting to secure a permanent territory, until 407 when he was appointed general by Honorius as part of a western attempt to annex the Balkans. The planned campaign was cancelled, relations between Alaric and Honorius deteriorated, and Alaric invaded Italy again to secure payment for his contracted services. While negotiating with Honorius at Ravenna about territory, alliance, and payments of gold and corn, Alaric besieged Rome. Honorius procrastinated, but in 409 the threat of starvation forced the senate at Rome to agree terms; Alaric had the senator Attalus proclaimed emperor and Attalus appointed Alaric as senior Roman general.

Tensions between Attalus and Alaric, plus further unsuccessful negotiations with Honorius, resulted in Alaric returning to Rome, which was easily captured on 24 August 410. Occupation of the city for three days may have relieved Alaric's frustrations, but did not satisfy his followers' needs for territory. Thereafter he led his forces south, with North Africa as his probable goal, but was thwarted while trying to cross to Sicily; as he withdrew northwards he became ill and died. His brother-in-law Athaulf took over the army, which he led into southern Gaul in 412 where

Theodoric's mausoleum at Ravenna. Constructed from Istrian marble, with the dome formed from a single block weighing 300 tons, this projected Theoderic's ambition to create a lasting regime. (Ancient Art and Architecture)

the Visigothic kingdom was established in Aquitania.

Theoderic, Ostrogothic king

Theoderic was born in the mid-fifth century into the Amal family which led one of the Gothic groups in the northern Balkans. In 461/2 he was sent as hostage to Constantinople, where he remained for 10 years, receiving his education. After succeeding his father in 474, he spent 15 years attempting to establish a base for his people in the Balkans, either through negotiation with or intimidation of the eastern emperor Zeno. Theoderic's successes were marked by appointments as Roman general in 476/8 and again 483–87, when Zeno employed him against other tribesmen

in the Balkans as well as Isaurian rebels in the east. Rebuffs resulted in the sacking of cities, such as Stobi in 479, or the ravaging of provinces, for example Macedonia and Thessaly in 482.

Theoderic writes to Emperor Anastasius protesting his loyalty; the letter illustrates a tribal warlord's attachment to the ideal of Rome (Cassiodorus, Variae 1.1).

'Our royalty is an imitation of yours, modelled on your good purpose, a copy of the only Empire; and in so far as we follow you do we excel all other nations. Often you have exhorted me to love the senate, to accept cordially the laws of past emperors, to join together in one all the members of Italy. How can you separate from your august alliance one whose character you thus try to make conformable to your own? There is moreover that noble sentiment, love for the city of Rome, from which two princes, both of whom govern in her name, should never be disjoined.'

The death of his main Gothic rival, Theoderic Strabo, in 481 allowed Theoderic to unite most Balkan Goths under Amal leadership, but he was still unable to achieve his main goal of acquiring a secure and productive territory. In 488 Zeno agreed that Theoderic should move to Italy to attack Odoacer (who had ruled since deposing the last western emperor in 476): if successful, Theoderic could rule on behalf of Zeno. Theoderic forced Odoacer back into Ravenna; after three years of blockade the rivals agreed to share power, but Theoderic soon accused Odoacer of treachery and had him killed. Zeno's death in 491 complicated Theoderic's position, but in 497 Emperor Anastasius recognised him as ruler of Italy; to his Gothic followers Theoderic was king, even sometimes Augustus (emperor), the status to which he clearly aspired, although he was careful to protest his subservience in dealings with Constantinople.

Theoderic's 33-year reign (493–526) came to be regarded as a golden age in Italy, especially in contrast to the fighting of the 540s, and his first two decades were highly successful. Marital diplomacy built links with the main tribal groups in the west, and from 507 brought the Visigothic kingdom in Spain under his control. The senate and Pope at Rome were courted by special treatment and the carefully crafted Roman image of the new regime; religious divisions between Rome and Constantinople facilitated this rapprochement. For Goths Theoderic remained the war leader, but this was now only one facet of his complex public image. Theoderic's last decade was less rosy. The absence of a son, and the early death of his son-in-law raised the issue of succession, while Anastasius' death in 518 brought religious reconciliation between Rome and Constantinople and so made Theoderic more suspicious of leading Romans. Theoderic's death in 526 rapidly brought to the surface the tensions within his kingdom, which Belisarius' invasion was to exploit.

Narses, imperial eunuch and trusted general

The eunuch Narses originated from the Persian part of Armenia but was brought up in the palace at Constantinople in the late fifth century. He advanced through the grades of servants of the Bedchamber, reaching the position of treasurer and senior official in 530/1; in this capacity he provided money to Persarmenian deserters, and travelled to the east to secure valuable booty. In 531/2 he became imperial sword-bearer, and on 18 January 532 his distribution of bribes was crucial in undermining the cohesion of rioters in Constantinople whose violence was threatening to topple Emperor Justinian. In 535 he undertook another delicate mission, this time for Empress Theodora, to reinstate Bishop Theodosius at Alexandria and exile his opponents; for over a year Narses remained in Alexandria, conducting a virtual civil war against Theodosius' opponents.

The Barberini ivory probably showing Emperor Justinian.
Above Christ blesses the emperor, who is honoured by a
victory to his left while a defeated easterner stands
behind his spear and other easterners offer gifts below.
To one side a general offers a statue of victory and
Earth displays her bounty beneath the horse's hooves.
(AKG London/Erich Lessing)

In 538, at nearly 60 years old, Narses
embarked on what was to prove a highly
successful military career by leading
reinforcements to Belisarius in Italy. Narses
criticised Belisarius' conduct, and their
rivalry led to the loss of Milan. Narses was
recalled to Constantinople, to be followed by
the allied contingent of Heruls, who refused
to remain without him. In 541/2 Narses was
again employed on sensitive business, first to
spy on an alleged plot that involved
Justinian's senior financial minister and then
to investigate unrest in Constantinople. In

545 his contacts among the Heruls were exploited to persuade their leaders to enrol for service in Italy.

Narses' big chance came in 551, after Belisarius had failed to stabilise the military position in Italy and Justinian's first choice as replacement (his nephew Germanus) had died. Narses was now appointed supreme commander in Italy, a post he accepted on condition that he was provided with the men and money needed to finish the war. Assembly of troops and other preparations detained Narses in the Balkans, and he did not arrive in Ravenna until 6 June 552 after outmanoeuvring Gothic contingents blocking the main routes. Later that month Narses marched against the Goths' leader Totila, whose various attempts at deception he outwitted and whom he then crushed in battle through intelligent tactics. In July Narses rapidly recaptured Rome before confronting the Goths near Naples. Clever planning again secured victory, although contemporaries also gave credit to Narses' devotion to the Virgin Mary.

For the next decade Narses was occupied in reducing Gothic strongholds in central and northern Italy and defeating Frankish invasions. Meanwhile he was entrusted by Justinian with the massive task of returning Italy to civilian rule, as well as ensuring adherence to the emperor's preferred religious doctrines. By 559 he had received the title of patrician, the Empire's highest honour, and by 565 he had also become honorary consul, a demonstration of his place in the traditional Roman hierarchy. Justinian's death in 565 complicated Narses' last decade, as his relations with Justin II were naturally less close. The migration of Lombards into the Po valley from 568 posed new military challenges, but he remained in post until his death in 573/4, at the age of almost 95.

Shahvaraz, Persian general and usurper

Farrukhan was a Persian Christian, nicknamed Shahvaraz, 'wild boar', by King Khusro II for his energy in attacking the Romans. In 614 he overran Palestine and captured Jerusalem after a bloody siege; he dispatched the surviving Christian population into captivity in Babylonia, along with the relic of the True Cross, although other lesser relics such as the Holy Sponge and Lance were presented to Emperor Heraclius. Over the next three years he organised the capture of Egypt, and then from 622 campaigned in Asia Minor as Heraclius marshalled the Roman counter-offensive. Heraclius had the better of their manoeuvring and engagements, but in 626 Shahvaraz advanced to the Bosporus where he attempted to assist the Avars' attack on Constantinople. Roman naval power prevented him from crossing to Europe, but after the Avar withdrawal he remained at Chalcedon. Apparently Khusro tried to have him assassinated at this time, but the plan was uncovered (allegedly with Heraclius' help) and Shahvaraz refused to commit his army against the Romans.

In 628 Shahvaraz's sons supported the overthrow of Khusro, but in 630 he secured Heraclius' support for a coup against the young Ardashir. Shahvaraz, whose army was still occupying the eastern provinces, agreed to withdraw from Roman territory and return the relic of the Holy Cross. Shahvaraz only survived for two months as king before being murdered. His son Nicetas, whose name suggests an attachment to the family of Heraclius, commanded Roman troops against the Arabs in Syria in the 630s, but was executed by the caliph Umar in 641 after offering to subdue Persia for the Arabs.

Impact of conflict

Administration

Prolonged warfare was not a novelty for the Romans; indeed during their expansion they had almost prided themselves on the regularity of their involvement. But repeated campaigning inside the Roman Empire, with the consequent ravaging of estates, destruction of cities, and death or capture of civilians was unusual: before the frontier problems of the mid-third century, the civil wars of AD 69–70 and 193–97 had been the only serious instances; Hannibal's invasion of Italy in the late third century BC is the nearest parallel for such damage being inflicted by a foreigner. The new situation affected the Empire's organisation, economic and social structures, and systems of belief.

Military need prompted a fundamental change in government, from a single emperor to the collegiate rule which emerged under Diocletian. Subsequent emperors who had the opportunity to rule alone, for example Constantius II and Valentinian I, chose to appoint a colleague to share the burden of command: regional armies and provincial populations had greater confidence when an emperor was on hand. However, having multiple rulers could create tensions, as happened between Constans and Constantius II or Arcadius and Honorius; the most serious case of full-blown conflict between accepted colleagues, after Julian's proclamation in 360, was averted by Constantius' death. Even in the fifth century, when the greater problems and clearer separation of the two halves might have reduced co-operation, the east sent help to the west when possible. Imperial proliferation had administrative consequences: Diocletian's three colleagues,

and then Constantine's three sons, needed their own officials, with the result that the praetorian prefecture split into regional units.

Administrative units were also divided because of pressure from below. In the third century the financial problems caused by repeated invasion and rapid imperial turnover meant that new ways had to be devised to pay and supply the armies. As the value and regularity of traditional sources of tax revenue declined, so it seems that armies were increasingly encouraged to take affairs into their own hands and secure necessary supplies and other resources: instead of monetary taxation being extracted from provinces and delivered to the legions, who would then return much of it to the provinces through purchase of commodities, the armies short-circuited the process by taking what they needed in kind while leaving provincials to offset this against tax liabilities. Under Diocletian the state caught up with this process and acted to institutionalise it.

There had also been a long-term tendency for legions to be divided into smaller operational units whose separate existence gradually solidified as they became accustomed to campaigning and being quartered away from their parent legions. Dispersal of concentrations of legions and the attachment of units to provincial cities also facilitated problems of supply, while this distribution of troops also offered wider security when frontier defences no longer excluded invaders. These developments meant that soldiers had closer and more regular interaction with civilians, while the logistics of the tax system became more cumbersome as agricultural produce had to be gathered and stored.

A law of the early 370s illustrating some of the problems in accounting for official supplies (Theodosian Code 7.4.16).

'If the military accountants should not deliver at once at the end of a period of 30 days their original requisitions, they shall be compelled to restore from their own property, either to the soldiers themselves or to the fiscal storehouses the supplies which they failed to withdraw from the fiscal stores or which they omitted to issue to the service units whose accounts they kept.'

The traditional system of provincial government, which relied heavily on the participation of local urban elites, could not cope. This was partly because of the complexity of the changes, but more importantly the position of local elites was being undermined by the economic and military developments which surrounded them. Inflation and the decline in value of coinage meant that they had less wealth to spend in their cities, while invasion and civil war might destroy the agricultural prosperity on which aristocrats and cities alike depended; in the worst cases even fortified cities might be sacked. The vitality of cities declined and their elites, who remained wealthy through possession of land, might decide that it was better to withdraw to their estates rather than spend limited resources on sustaining an urban lifestyle. There was an interlocking cycle of urban impoverishment and decay, so that it was harder for cities to play their expected part in imperial government at the very moment when administrative demands were becoming greater.

One result was an increase, approximately twofold under Diocletian, in the number of provinces: if provincial elites could not perform their traditional functions, it was necessary for governors to be more closely involved in supervising tax collection and local justice. This encroachment of imperial governors on customary spheres of operation for local aristocrats further undermined the latter's authority and contributed to the cycle of decline mentioned above.

Provincial cities – one of the glories of the early Roman Empire whose extensive remains still dominate our perception of the classical Mediterranean world – came under increasing threat as their governing class became less interested in exercising local control. Leading locals could secure more power for themselves by entering the central administration, whose expansion at all levels from the provinces to the imperial courts required more educated participants. Instead of competition for municipal office, service to individual cities often became a chore for local aristocrats whose performance was bolstered by frequent imperial legislation; where this failed, tasks had to be overseen by appointees of the provincial governor, a further extension of central power and erosion of local pride. Ironically one factor which contributed to the continued importance of cities was military insecurity, since urban defences provided refuge for the inhabitants of the surrounding countryside, but this offered only a partial balance. If the threat became too intense or persisted too long, the cities would be in danger of succumbing and the local population, inevitably led by their richest, and hence most mobile members, contemplated flight.

The desertion of parts of the Empire emerged as a problem during the third century when repeated invasions depopulated considerable regions along the Rhine and Danube frontiers. The more fortunate inhabitants would have slipped away southwards, thereby contributing to the increased prosperity in late antiquity of south-western Gaul and the southern Balkans, but the majority either perished or were captured. These developments contributed to the Empire's tax problems, since certain areas produced little or nothing, while it took time to recognise the increased potential of other areas. In theory, the process of regular censuses to update tax registers instituted by Diocletian should have coped with such movements, but the

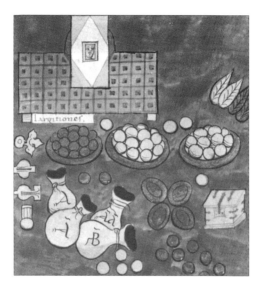

Folio from the *Notitia Dignitatum* showing the office of the *Count of the Sacred Largesses*, displaying, in addition to the standard letter of appointment, different forms of wealth for distribution. (MS Canon Misc. 378, f. 142v, Bodleian Library)

thorough reassessment of even one province was such a major undertaking that the crucial lists could not remain accurate. In practice the easiest way to make up for shortages in revenue was to squeeze accessible producers harder, both through increasing the standard tax demand and by imposing supplementary superindictions.

In some parts of the Empire the tax burden at times was probably excessive, which encouraged people to try to evade their dues. The richest and most powerful could ignore demands, while waiting for an emperor to announce one of the periodic cancellations of arrears. The poor and weak did so either by placing themselves under the protection of a rich neighbour who might (in return for payment or service of some sort) exercise his powers of obstruction for these new clients, or by moving to a new region to escape official notice. These developments prompted imperial legislation that attempted to tie people to their places of work: thus many types of urban craftsmen and shopkeepers became, in legal theory, hereditary

occupations, and in the countryside agricultural tenants were repeatedly decreed to be tied to their estates, although the frequent need for legislation suggests that the process was not all that easy.

Warlords

However complex the economic and administrative problems which protracted warfare caused, the Empire managed to survive the crisis of the third century to flourish for much of the fourth century. In the east this prosperity continued into the sixth century, but the western Empire relapsed into a cycle – ultimately fatal – of shrinking revenues and declining power during the fifth century. Invaders ravaged and depopulated large areas, but this time the damage extended much deeper into the Empire. The inability of the imperial government to repel groups such as the Visigoths led to their settlement, with official agreement, in productive provinces: south-western Gaul, much of Spain and finally, and most crucially, North Africa, passed out of Roman control. In some cases, such as the allocation of south-west Gaul to the Visigoths, the Empire in theory gained a powerful contingent of soldiers; in practice this resource could only be used when it suited the Visigoths themselves, as for example in a series of campaigns into Spain which ultimately benefited the Visigoths, and on other occasions emperors had to act against their nominal allies.

One important consequence of reductions in imperial power, perceived as well as real, was the emergence of local warlords who would control and defend particular areas against external pressures, both central and foreign. On occasions this happened with imperial consent: in the fifth century western emperors relaxed legislation against the carrying of arms by private individuals, an admission that taxation no longer bought safety. The Roman 'withdrawal' from the British Isles in 410 was probably such an incident, with the removal of the last official

Roman troops being accompanied by an exhortation to the Romano-British provincials to attend to their own defence. More often such developments occurred despite imperial wishes. At worst a powerful provincial warlord might come to be regarded as emperor, as was the case with Odaenathus of Palmyra, the separate Gallic emperors of the later third century, and Carausius in Britain; from the perspective of the imperial centre, these men were usurpers who had to be crushed when conditions permitted. When Roman rule was disintegrating similar rulers, such as Syagrius in northern Gaul in the 460s, could be seen as resolute champions of Roman authority.

Most warlords were less powerful and more local than such grand figures. They provide one plausible way of understanding the phenomenon of *bacaudae*, peasant brigands, who are said to have dominated parts of Gaul and Spain for limited periods between the third and fifth centuries. Rather than being class warriors keen to overthrow their landlords and the Roman state, they were probably an alliance of different inhabitants of a particular region ranging from poor tenants to local aristocrats, with the latter providing leadership. Such groups could easily move in and out of formal attachment to the Empire, as illustrated by the Isaurians, inhabitants of the mountains of southern Turkey. In the fourth century they revolted intermittently, probably when the ties binding local Isaurian leaders to the cities of neighbouring regions broke down. In the fifth century Isaurians came to be recognised as a precious military resource, being recruited into imperial service by Zeno, an Isaurian who became consul, senior general and patrician. In the next generation, through their domination of the imperial bodyguard, their leader, another Zeno, became son-in-law of Emperor Leo and eventually his successor. Their fall from favour after Emperor Zeno's death in 491 prompted a return to regional revolt, with even an attempt to proclaim a rival emperor.

Emperors had to strike a balance between tolerating the existence of such powerful local barons and dissipating their own

Charietto came to prominence in the early 350s as a tribal supporter of the western usurper Magnentius, but after the latter's defeat and death he had to sustain himself as a brigand. In 355 Julian, the newly appointed western Caesar, decided it was best to reach an accommodation with him. Charietto became a feared defender of the Rhine frontier, surviving Julian's departure to the east to die in action against invading Alamanni in 365, by which time he held the rank of count.

strength in attempts to discipline them. Many of the most important figures in the Empire had their personal retinues of supporters, most visibly in the form of the *bucellarii* who surrounded leading generals, but also in the monks or other ecclesiastical attendants in the entourage of major bishops and the lance-wielding guards for Anatolian estate owners whose misdeeds Justinian tried to regulate. These developments entailed that emperors did not have a monopoly of violence: a bishop of Alexandria could intimidate a general church council and prevent imperial officers from achieving their wishes, while at home his supporters might dismember a rival bishop and overawe imperial troops attempting to restore order. Legislation was meant to restrict such behaviour, but compromise was often easier; we find estates in Egypt which maintained their own groups of *bucellarii* and had private gaols. It was cheaper to uphold imperial authority in collaboration with such people, even if this effectively reduced the overall supremacy of the individual emperor.

The leaders of tribal groups who established themselves in Roman provinces could be placed in this category of warlords, effective military protectors whose authority gradually came to be accepted by remaining Roman inhabitants, even aristocrats, as well as their tribal followers. Visigothic and Ostrogothic kings had to maintain two contrasting images, as civilised dispensers of

In response to the Vandal conquest of Africa, Valentinian relaxed the ban on private individuals carrying weapons (June 440) (Valentinian III, Novel 6.2.3).

'As often as the public welfare demands we consider that the solicitude of all must be summoned in aid ... we admonish each and all by this edict that, with confidence in Roman strength, if the occasion should so demand, they shall use those arms which they can, but they shall preserve the public discipline and the moderation of free birth unimpaired.'

laws whose ability to uphold local peace justified their appropriation of properties which had once been Roman and of tax revenues, and as effective war leaders who could still circulate gifts to their entourages. Latin rhetoric, as seen through the writings of Cassiodorus, and Roman law as in the Code of Euric underpinned the former aspect. On the other hand, the continuing importance of military prowess contributed to a militarisation of the Roman elements in their kingdoms: in Merovingian France and Visigothic Spain in the sixth century the surviving Roman cities maintained their own militias which could be quite effective, if small, military units.

Christianity

War fundamentally affected the Empire in a variety of ways, but perhaps the development of greatest long-term significance was its impact on religious beliefs; war and victory underpinned the explosion of Christianity as the Empire's dominant religion. In the third century the traditional Graeco-Roman gods oversaw the salvation of the Empire, aided in accordance with individual preference by a variety of other local or imported deities such as Mithras or the Unconquered Sun. Worship was an important factor in ensuring the allegiance and discipline of the armies, as illustrated by the calendar of religious sacrifices from Dura Europus (the Roman outpost on the Euphrates): the life of military units was organised around a series of sacrifices, in which commemoration of important imperial anniversaries was prominent, while images of the current emperor or emperors were placed between the legionary standards so that they shared the fierce loyalty which the eagles attracted. The major persecutions of Christians in the third century were triggered by imperial demands to sacrifice for the safety of the Empire.

The religious world changed, at least in outward appearance, when Constantine adopted the Christian God as his divine companion and granter of victory, a move justified by successes at the Milvian Bridge and then over Licinius. Thereafter the Christian God assisted his servants, whether in civil war as at Mursa in 351 when Constantius' victory was signalled by the appearance of a cross in the sky at Jerusalem, or in foreign adventures as in Justinian's reconquest of Africa, which was guaranteed by a bishop's dream and Christian omens. Emperors might consult prominent Christians about future campaigns, as when Zeno visited Daniel the Stylite, who had taken up residence on a column near the Bosporus, to ask his advice about an expedition to fight the Vandals. The Church became involved in victory celebrations to the extent that the victorious entry of Justinian to Constantinople in 559 culminated in prayers at the altar of S. Sophia. Imperial warfare might even take on crusading overtones: Constantine's final campaign against Persia was accompanied by propaganda about the liberation of Christians in Mesopotamia, and in the 620s Heraclius mobilised the rump of his Empire to ward off Persians and Avars by presenting the Romans as the beleaguered children of Israel with a mission to crush the heathen and recover the relic of the Holy Cross from Babylon.

In contrast to such successes, non-Christians were spectacularly unsuccessful:

Ankara citadel. (Author's collection)

Julian the apostate led a massive army to disaster in Persia, while his own death in a skirmish was attributed by some to the miraculous intervention of St Mercurius; the pagan usurper Eugenius was overwhelmed by the orthodox Theodosius at the Frigidus River; and Constantinople was delivered from the threat of an alleged Gothic plot by the intervention of an angel. Heretical Christians might be as unsuccessful: Emperor Valens, an opponent of Nicene Christianity, died after the catastrophe of Adrianople.

Everything conspired to demonstrate the power of the true Christian God and the importance of correct worship, an issue which had already exercised Constantine: he urged the importance of Christian unity to achieve efficacious supplications to God and provided support for clergy attached to the correct, orthodox, group. As a result, emperors became closely involved in the agreement and enforcement of what was doctrinally right, and in ecclesiastical discipline, although these areas of belief proved much more resistant to Imperial

command than the secular fields in which they usually operated. Within months of his victory at the Milvian Bridge, Constantine was invited to adjudicate in the Donatist dispute – which originated in challenges to the legitimacy of North African clergy who had not stood up to persecution in the third century – and a year after defeating Licinius and acquiring the eastern Empire he presided at the universal council of Nicaea, which attempted to resolve the Arian dispute about the relationship of God the Father and Christ the Son. In each case the dispute was still unresolved a century later.

Emperors used their full military might and political power to uphold their authority over the Church, but it was difficult to achieve the intended results. Justinian had Pope Vigilius brought to Constantinople and then forcibly wrenched from the altar where he had taken refuge to attend a church council in 553, but the Emperor's doctrinal statement which resulted was not widely accepted in the west for over 50 years. In Constantinople occasional tensions between emperor and bishop exacerbated the perennial problems of maintaining order in major conurbations: when Arcadius had Bishop John Chrysostom arrested in 404, the attendant rioting resulted in the burning of S. Sophia and the Senate; Bishop Chrysostom died in exile in 407, but a generation later he was accepted as one of the pillars of the Greek Church.

Alexandria was even more out of control, since the city's bishops financed an enormous clerical establishment, including hundreds of monks in the nearby desert who could be brought into the city and mobilised as needed. Emperors did not regularly keep enough troops in Egypt to confront this potent combination of force, bribery and patronage, and it was easier to come to an accommodation with the preferred leader of the Egyptian Church. Even when emperors resolved to intervene, the authority of their ecclesiastical nominees rarely extended beyond the city of Alexandria, and their opponents were always awaiting the opportunity to strike back: Proterius was sustained as bishop with Emperor Marcian's backing, but on Marcian's death he was dragged from the baptistery of his church and publicly dismembered by supporters of his rival, Timothy the Cat.

Although Christianity often confirmed imperial prestige, the Church could not fail to be involved also in the fragmentation of authority in the Empire. This was partly because of the power of the bishop in local society. The bishop of Alexandria was exceptional in absolute terms, but in most of the Empire's cities the local bishop was a leading property owner and patron, as well as a person of education. As such they were often trusted to represent their cities: in 481 the bishop of Heraclea in Macedonia saved his people by providing food for Theoderic's Goths; during Khusro I's invasion of Syria in 540 bishops attempted to negotiate limits to Persian depredations; and requests to an emperor for tax remission after a natural disaster might well be articulated by the bishop. This authority, however, could also threaten imperial interests: at Thessalonica in 481, the inhabitants rioted at a rumour that Emperor Zeno intended to allow Goths

to settle in the city and removed the keys from the imperial prefect to entrust them to the bishop; in 594 the bishop of Asemus near the Danube prevented the local militia from being conscripted into the mobile army commanded by Emperor Maurice's brother.

Communities might come to look to living saints or relics as well as bishops to protect them in the absence of imperial help. In the fragmenting western Empire of the fifth century, St Genevieve was credited with saving Paris from Attila, while at Clermont Ferrand in the 470s Bishop Sidonius introduced new devotions to sustain local morale during a protracted blockade. The development of the story of Christ's protection for Edessa in Mesopotamia has already been noted (see page 56). Thessalonica is another place where one can see the local church developing its supernatural assistants when imperial protection was lacking. In the early seventh century the city's bishop produced a collection of miracles performed by the city's patron saint Demetrius, which particularly stressed his ability to save his city from capture by Avars and Slavs; the collection was designed for public recitation during a renewed bout of Avar pressure. Later in the century, when the city was virtually cut off from Constantinople and imperial support, the collection was expanded with further examples of Demetrius' miraculous intervention in sieges and blockades. Demetrius was capable of humbling imperial prefects who did not recognise his superior authority or attend to the interests of his city, and of challenging the emperor by redirecting food supplies bound for Constantinople.

As long as the Empire flourished the close connection of Christianity and war strengthened imperial authority, and even the occasions of tension when secular power was fragmenting reflected rather than caused imperial decline. There are, however, ways in which the Church has been criticised for contributing to the Empire's collapse, through the appropriation of

The walls of Nicaea, (modern Iznik, Turkey); the column bases and other reused material at the bases of the towers reflects their rapid construction. (Author's collection)

precious resources and the inculcation of an unwarlike or defeatist spirit.

The Church did require the service of numerous clergy, and the growing monastic

The importance of the secular role of bishops is illustrated in the explanation for the choice of a new bishop at Antioch in 527, shortly after the city had been struck by a massive earthquake (Evagrius, Ecclesiastical History 4.6).

'At the very moment of despair God raised up Ephrem, the Count of the east, to assume every care that the city of Antioch should not lack any necessities. As a consequence the Antiochenes, in admiration, elected him as their priest and he obtained the apostolic see as a reward for his especial support.'

importantly, as a recipient of benefactions individual churches accumulated massive wealth in precious metal. How far these developments drained secular resources depends in part on the costs of religious activities in the period before the triumph of Christianity, but there is likely to have been an increase. In a crisis monks and clergy might be made liable to conscription, and ecclesiastical treasures were often deployed to ransom captives or save cities from being sacked; in the 620s Heraclius financed his campaigns through a compulsory loan of the wealth of the church at Constantinople. This might suggest that these resources were not completely alienated from secular use, but the question must remain as to whether they might have been employed more effectively if they had been available to finance regular military expenditure.

With regard to attitudes towards war it is essential not to impose modern views: for us Christianity might be a religion of peace, but Constantine had chosen the Christians' deity as an Old Testament God of Battles. There was, however, a negative side to Christianity's ability to sustain Roman morale, since the belief that God rewarded his virtuous servants with victory also provided an explanation for defeat in terms of sin or incorrect worship. In the eastern empire during the sixth century a long-running dispute about the composition

movement in the fifth century removed many more from secular activities. As a massive property owner, the Church reduced the area liable to taxation and, more

Walls of Thessalonica, the fourth-century defences of Galerius' capital. (Author's collection)

of Christ, how the divine and human elements were fused within his single being without undermining the integrity of either element, resulted in the alienation from Constantinople of many of the inhabitants of the eastern provinces. Emperors were regarded as heretical, and attempts to coerce unity as persecution. As a result imperial misfortune came to be expected, or at least accepted by the populations of Syria, Egypt and Armenia who did not share the emperor's views. The situation became even more complex in the 630s when Heraclius attempted to impose a doctrinal compromise which most Christians found unacceptable: the emperor's descent into heresy provided the perfect explanation for the contemporary successes of the Arabs. Nothing was likely to be achieved until the emperor turned back to God and worshipped correctly, so nothing should be done.

Notable individuals

Ambrose, Bishop of Milan

Ambrose (bishop 374–97), son of a praetorian prefect, pursued an official career and became governor of the province of Aemilia in 372/3, with his seat at Milan, the western imperial capital. The Church at Milan was dominated by Arians with imperial support when Ambrose got involved, somewhat improperly, in the election of a new bishop for the supporters of the Council of Nicaea. Ambrose was chosen, though he was not yet baptised, so that he progressed to the bishopric one week after formally joining the Church.

Ambrose energetically promoted his brand of Christianity, building churches and discovering relics to underpin their sanctity, promoting female piety, encouraging hymn singing and patronising scholarship. He was an accomplished orator, whose intellectual sermons gained a following among educated imperial officials, people of similar background to him. His secular career gave him the skills to manipulate councils into supporting his views, and the experience to stand up to emperors, first Valentinian II, who demanded a church for Arian worship, then, twice, Theodosius over his attempt to punish zealous Christians in Syria who had destroyed a synagogue and his massacre of civilians in Thessalonica; on the last occasion the emperor performed public penance. Ambrose, however, also used Christianity to uphold imperial power, being responsible for linking the legend of the discovery of the True Cross to Constantine's mother, Helena: Ambrose

Stylised woodcut showing a scene from the life of Ambrose, Bishop of Milan. (Ancient Art and Architecture)

proposed that the incorporation of nails from the Cross into the imperial helmet and bridle symbolised Christianity's support for enduring secular military authority. After his death in 397, Ambrose's reputation was rapidly consolidated through a biography by his secretary, but the bishopric of Milan lost its special importance when the court moved to the greater safety of Ravenna.

Symeon, ascetic and saint

Symeon Stylites (390–459) was one of the most influential of eastern holy men. After a decade in various Syrian monasteries where his fierce asceticism provoked unease, Symeon moved to a hillside near Telneshin where he lived in a small hut; fame brought pilgrims whose attentions prompted Symeon to transfer first to one column, and then to a taller one of about 60 feet (20.4m) where he remained for the last 30 years of his life. The power of his prayers and curses was famous and attracted visitors from the west and beyond the Empire's borders. Symeon berated Emperor Theodosius II for legislating to protect law-abiding pagans and Jews, and Emperor Leo consulted him in 457 about sensitive ecclesiastical issues.

Symeon's death on 2 September 459 provoked competition for his body and relics: his companions feared that local villagers or nomadic Arabs might steal his corpse for their own benefit. Martyrius, patriarch of Antioch, and Ardabur, the senior general in the east, came to the column with Gothic soldiers who escorted the corpse to Antioch, where the inhabitants wanted it as a talisman against earthquakes; Symeon, too, looked after himself by freezing Martyrius' hand when the latter attempted to remove a hair from his beard. Symeon's dirty leather loincloth was offered to Emperor Leo, but ended up in the possession of Symeon's spiritual son, the stylite Daniel, who took up his station on the Bosporus. During the 480s a massive monastic complex was constructed at Qalat Seman around Symeon's empty column, the main church being 328 feet (100m) from east to west and

The historian Evagrius records an occasion in the 580s when the senior general in the east asked to use Symeon's relics (1.13).

'I saw his holy head when Philippicus requested that precious relics be sent for the protection of the eastern armies. And the extraordinary thing was that the hairs which lay upon his head had not been corrupted, but are preserved as if he were alive again. And the skin on his forehead was wrinkled and withered, but still it is intact, as are the majority of his teeth, except for those forcibly removed by the hands of devout men.'

295 feet (90m) from north to south, and the site remained a popular focus for pilgrimage.

John the Lydian, eastern civil servant

John was born in 490 at Philadelphia in Asia Minor, from where he moved to Constantinople to find a post in the palace secretariat. While awaiting an opening he studied philosophy, but then jumped at the opportunity provided by the elevation of a fellow-townsman to the praetorian prefecture in 511. He was allocated a senior position with a substantial income from semi-official fees, and rewarded for a panegyric of his patron with one gold coin per line. John had an excellent knowledge of Latin, which was being used less commonly in the eastern Empire, even though it was the language of law, and for a time he was very busy preparing legal materials in the prefecture while also maintaining an alternative career path by working in the palace. After his patron left office, John's career reverted to a more normal trajectory whereby length of service determined promotion.

John's literary talents continued to attract attention, and he was asked by Justinian to present a panegyric in front of aristocrats from Rome and then to compose a history of the Persian campaigns including the Roman victory at Dara in 530. He secured one of the public professorships in Constantinople, probably in the 540s, and combined this with work in the prefecture until his retirement after 40 years and four months of service in 551/2. He is best known for his work 'On Magistracies', which included a study of the praetorian prefecture that aired his own jaundiced views on administrative innovations and the declining importance of traditional qualities, such as literary ability and skill at Latin.

Cassiodorus, Roman in Ostrogothic service

Three generations of Cassiodori had been important public officials in Italy for Roman and tribal rulers when the young Flavius Magnus Aurelius Cassiodorus Senator was selected by his father, the praetorian prefect, as advisor in 503–07. Thereafter he regularly served the Ostrogoths at Ravenna as legal expert and composer of official correspondence in elegant Latin, along the way securing the honours of a consulship in 514 and the

Folio from the *Notitia Dignitatum* showing the office of the praetorian prefect with ceremonial four-horse carriage, ink stand, candlesticks, and imperial letter of appointment. (MS Canon Misc. 378, f. 90, Bodleian Library)

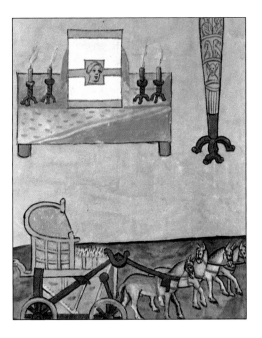

patriciate in the 530s; even after the start of the Justinianic reconquest he continued to serve as praetorian prefect, organising supplies for Ostrogothic forces. With the collapse of the Ostrogothic regime he embraced the religious life, and was in Constantinople in 550, probably as a refugee from the war-torn chaos of Italy. In the mid-550s he returned to found a monastery at Squillace in his native Calabria, where he lived until his death in about 580.

He was a prolific writer. Apart from the 12 volumes of letters which underpin our knowledge of the Ostrogothic kingdom, he composed panegyrics on King Theoderic and his son-in-law, accepted a royal request to write a history of the Goths which proclaimed the antiquity of the Gothic race and the ruling Amal family, and produced several philosophical and religious works. At his monastery he hoped that secular learning could be sustained as an aid to religious understanding; to this end he compiled two books of 'Divine and Human Institutes', works on grammar, etymology and figures of speech, which were intended to assist his monks in their role as scribes, and commentaries on the Psalms and other books of the Bible. In addition he commissioned other works, such as a Latin translation of the main Greek church historians of the fourth and fifth centuries. His monastery scarcely survived his death, but his writings had a profound influence on the direction of western monasticism and its role in the preservation of classical learning.

Antonina, wife of general Belisarius

Antonina was born probably about 484, into a family of entertainers, her father being a charioteer in Constantinople and her mother an actress. She had at least one husband before marrying Belisarius, sometime in the early 520s when he was bodyguard for the future Emperor Justinian; if one believes the historian Procopius (who disliked Antonina) she had previously had several lovers and betrayed Belisarius by pursuing an affair with his godson.

Promotion for Belisarius and friendship with Justinian's wife, Empress Theodora – another product of the entertainment world – brought Antonina considerable influence; at some point she was granted the exalted patrician rank. She accompanied Belisarius on his western campaigns, helping to improve the expedition's water supply on the voyage to Africa in 533, organising a fleet and supplies for Belisarius during the siege of Rome in 537, and allegedly dominating her husband. On behalf of Theodora she helped to oust Pope Silverius in 537, secure the downfall of Justinian's former financial officer John the Cappadocian in 541, and persuade Pope Vigilius to espouse Theodora's theological preferences. When Belisarius was disgraced in 542/3 Antonina worked to recover imperial favour, and then accompanied him on his reappointment to Italy in 544. She returned to Constantinople to plead for reinforcements, but the death of Theodora in 548 persuaded her to press instead for Belisarius' recall; she also terminated the marriage of her daughter to Theodora's grandson to prevent the imperial house from acquiring the family's wealth. She may have outlived Belisarius, who died in 565.

Ravenna mosaic of Theodora, wife of Justinian I, with her entourage. Mosaic from the Basilica of S. Vitale, Ravenna. (Ancient Art and Architecture)

Making new boundaries

Disintegration of the Empire

A period of war lasting four centuries and involving several different regional conflicts is unlikely to have a clear end, but three major developments can legitimately be considered to signal the conclusion of the campaigns of the late Roman period: in the eastern empire and North Africa the sweeping victories of Islamic Arabs; in the Balkans the progressive occupation of territory by Slav tribes, who eventually generated identifiable governing elites; and in the west the consolidation of tribal kingdoms in spite of Justinian's massive effort at reconquest.

In the east while Heraclius had been locked in his desperate struggle with the Persians, events of enormous importance were unfolding in the Arabian peninsula. At Mecca a 40-year-old trader received a divine message from the angel Gabriel. For the next dozen years or so Muhammad stayed in Mecca, receiving more messages, and gradually built up a following, although this success increased tensions with the polytheists who remained the majority community. In 622 Muhammad and his followers moved north to Yathrib (Medina), an event (the *hijra*) which marked the start of the Islamic era.

By Muhammad's death in 632 he had asserted his control over Mecca as well as much of the northern part of the Arabian peninsula, and under his successors the Arabs pushed into Palestine and Syria. In 633 and 634 there was a series of limited victories, which permitted the Arabs to enter Damascus. In 636 a major Roman counter-offensive, commanded by the Emperor Heraclius' brother Theodore who had assembled most of the military resources of the eastern provinces, ended in disaster at

the River Yarmuk. Roman resistance was broken and over the next few years the major cities of Palestine and Syria surrendered, while in 640 the Arabs took over Roman Mesopotamia and campaigned into Armenia, Cilicia and Anatolia. In 639 attacks on Egypt began and by 642 this province too was captured; in less than a decade all the richest areas of the Roman Empire had fallen under Arab control.

What is most striking about this achievement – apart from its speed and complete surprise – is that at the same time Arab armies were dismantling the Persian Empire. Admittedly the Sassanid dynasty had been in turmoil since Khusro II's overthrow in 628, but the accession of Khusro's grandson Yazdgard III in 632 had brought some stability; however, Persian armies were unable to withstand this new challenge. By the early 640s Yazdgard had been forced to abandon all the royal cities in lower Mesopotamia and seek refuge in north-eastern Iran; in 651 Yazdgard was under pressure even there when his assassination terminated the Sassanid dynasty and confirmed Muslim rule over the whole of the Middle East.

By 700 the Arabs had wrested all North Africa from Roman control, and had started to conquer the Visigoths in Spain. The one direction in which they failed to make lasting progress was in Anatolia, where Roman resistance gradually hardened. After capturing Alexandria the Arabs developed a powerful navy, which brought control of Cyprus and endangered the southern coastline of Asia Minor and the Aegean islands. On land, repeated raiding impoverished vast tracts of inland Asia Minor, and resulted in the destruction or desertion of many of the major cities: refugees streamed away from the invaders in

Islamic conquests

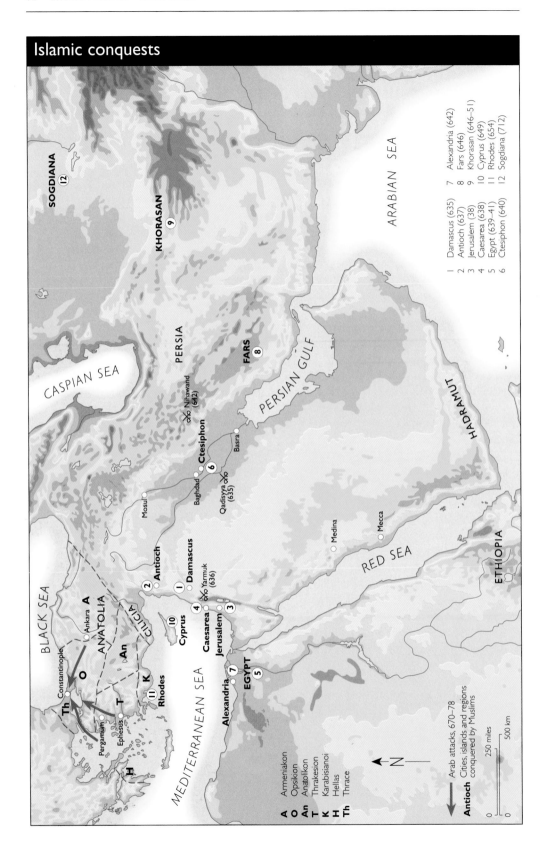

1 Damascus (635)
2 Antioch (637)
3 Jerusalem (38)
4 Caesarea (638)
5 Egypt (639–41)
6 Ctesiphon (640)
7 Alexandria (642)
8 Fars (646)
9 Khorasan (646–51)
10 Cyprus (649)
11 Rhodes (654)
12 Sogdiana (712)

A   Armeniakon
O   Opsikion
An   Anatolikon
T   Thrakesion
K   Karabisianoi
H   Hellas
Th   Thrace

Arab attacks, 670–78

Antioch Cities, islands and regions conquered by Muslims

0   250 miles
0   500 km

Post-Roman West

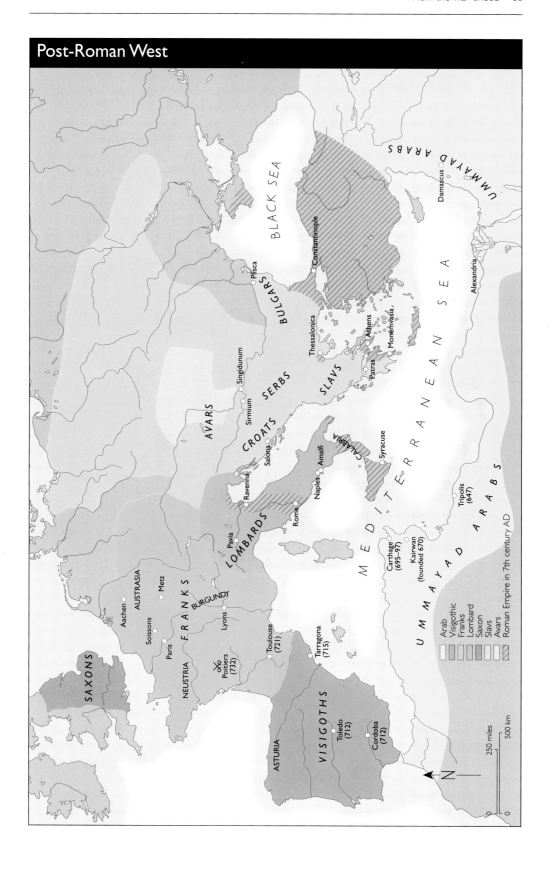

UMMAYAD ARABS

Damascus

BLACK SEA

Alexandria

Constantinople

Pliska

BULGARS

Thessalonica

Athens

Monemvasia

Patras

SERBS

Singidunum

AVARS

Sirmium

CROATS

SLAVS

CALABRIA

Salona

Syracuse

Ravenna

M E D I T E R R A N E A N   S E A

Naples Amalfi

Tripolis
(647)

Pavia

Rome

LOMBARDS

Carthage
(695–97)

Kairwan
(founded 670)

U M M A Y A D   A R A B S

Aachen

AUSTRASIA

Metz

FRANKS

BURGUNDY

Soissons

Lyons

Paris

Toulouse
(721)

Tarragona
(715)

NEUSTRIA

Poitiers
(732)

SAXONS

VISIGOTHS

Toledo
(712)

Cordoba
(712)

ASTURIA

Arab
Visigothic
Franks
Lombard
Saxon
Slavs
Avars
Roman Empire in 7th century AD

250 miles

500 km

N

0

search of safety in the mountains, while repeated disaster challenged the stability of religious convictions. At Constantinople, however, in the 670s, the Arabs eventually stumbled decisively: the capital's substantial walls and the Roman navy (with its secret weapon of Greek fire) were underpinned by the city's divine defenders, among whom the Virgin was prominent through the relics of her robe and girdle, and the Arabs were compelled to retreat.

Over the next generation a new order was created in Roman territory: the old social system based on the grand provincial cities had been swept away so that villages and rural markets came to the fore, while administrative organisation was directed towards sustaining the military units responsible for frontier defence. Only Constantinople survived as a recognisable city, and even its population had probably shrunk to a tenth of what it had once been. Continued failure to reverse Arab successes contributed to religious upheaval: for much of the eighth century the rump of the eastern Empire was riven by disputes about the validity of images in Christian worship, with iconoclast emperors supporting the Muslim view that images were idolatrous.

In the Balkans the Romans experienced losses which, if less spectacular in terms of military action, were almost as complete as

---

At Pergamum in 716 the defenders resorted to desperate measures, intended to avert an apocalyptic scourge (Theophanes, Chronographica *p.390).*

'Maslamah ben Abd al-Malik came to Pergamum, which he besieged and captured by God's dispensation, through the Devil's machinations. For at a magician's instigation the city's inhabitants procured a pregnant woman and cut her up; after removing the infant and cooking it in a pot, all those about to fight dipped the sleeves of their right arm in the loathsome sacrifice. Accordingly they were delivered to the enemy.'

---

in the east. We have no detailed knowledge of the sequence of events after Maurice's death in 602, when Roman authority had been superficially restored over much of the peninsula. Phocas and Heraclius both gave precedence to eastern campaigns; troops were progressively removed from the Balkans, which permitted Slav groups to move unhindered across the countryside. The Avars occasionally invaded to extend their authority over the Slavs and surviving Romans, but even their humiliation outside Constantinople in 626 brought no lasting respite. As the Avar federation disintegrated, smaller tribal groups emerged to dominate particular areas, the Bulgars in the north-east, and Croats and Serbs in the north-west. By the latter part of the seventh century only the hinterland of Constantinople and isolated enclaves at Thessalonica, Athens, Corinth and other places accessible by sea remained under Roman authority.

In the western state, the deposition of the last Roman emperor in 476 had brought one sort of end, with Vandals in control of Africa, Visigoths in Spain and southern Gaul, Merovingian Franks in northern Gaul and the Ostrogoths soon to arrive in Italy. Justinian's reconquest threatened to turn back the clock, but in the later sixth century it was the Romans who were being squeezed by the arrival of the Lombards in Italy and the reassertion of Visigothic power in Spain. The west was even lower down the list of imperial priorities than the Balkans, and little could be done to influence events: in 578 Emperor Tiberius had recognised this when he returned the gold which the Roman senate had sent as a gift for his accession with the advice that they should use this to purchase allies among the newly arrived Lombards. By the 590s Roman rule in Italy was confined to Ravenna in the north, which was precariously joined to another area around Rome, and from there to larger enclaves of the extreme south and Sicily. In the seventh century even the visit to Rome of Emperor Constans II did not conclusively re-establish Roman authority. Eventually a

Dome of the Rock, Jerusalem a symbol of Islamic
power at the centre of Christian and Jewish faiths.
(Ancient Art and Architecture)

from the south. These victories were accompanied by the conversion of their King Clovis, significantly to Catholic Christianity rather than the Arian beliefs which other Germanic tribes espoused; but partitive inheritance between competing branches of the family then disrupted the kingdom's unity. During the sixth century Clovis' successors had on various occasions intervened in Italy, on both sides of the Roman reconquest, contemplated a grand alliance of tribes to challenge Constantinople, resisted Avar encroachments in southern Germany, and weathered attempts from Constantinople to destabilise the dynastic balance between different parts of the kingdom.

A graffito scratched by one of the defenders of Sirmium during its three-year siege by the Avars in 579–82.
  'Lord Christ, help the city and smite the Avars and watch over Romania and the writer. Amen.'

combination of religious hostility to iconoclast developments in the east, lack of respect for the absent and unsuccessful emperors, and resistance to tax demands terminated east Roman control over Rome and Ravenna; the Roman Empire survived in Sicily and parts of the south, but had ceased to be a significant element in Italian affairs.

The most important events for the future of the west occurred in France. By the early sixth century this had been largely united under the Merovingian Frankish dynasty which had first suppressed Roman warlords in the north and then driven the Visigoths

After the 630s Merovingian rulers wielded little real power, which increasingly slipped into the hands of the royal stewards, the most powerful being the family of Pippin. By the late seventh century the Pippinids had effectively displaced the Merovingians and it was the Pippinid Charles Martel who rolled back the Islamic invaders at Poitiers in 732. Thereafter his grandson Charles 'the Great' – Charlemagne – reunited Frankish Gaul and conquered the Lombards in Italy. Charlemagne's visit to Rome in 800 and his coronation in St Peter's sealed the creation of the Holy Roman Empire.

Roman legacies

The four centuries of war during which the Roman Empire was torn apart provided the basis for a new political map of Europe, the Middle East and North Africa. Instead of a collection of provinces whose different peoples, cultures and traditions were gradually transformed through contact with Roman power so that acceptance of a central authority was accompanied by a display of some common features, a fragmented world emerged; in different areas diverse elites came to the fore, a process whose results still dominate the modern map.

The Roman Empire did not end, since the rump of the eastern provinces continued to be ruled from Constantinople by emperors who regarded themselves and their people as

The walls of Ankara showing the pentagonal tower. (Ancient Art and Architecture)

Rhomaioi. This beleaguered state, which saw itself as the guardian of the Roman political, religious and cultural inheritance, found the resources to survive the intense Arab pressure of the late seventh and early eighth centuries and then to embark on substantial reconquests in the Balkans and Asia Minor in the tenth. Although the arrival of the Seljuk Turks in the eleventh century curtailed its resources and power again, the fabled wealth of the east attracted Viking mercenaries to travel south through Russia, and then the treacherous Fourth Crusade sacked Constantinople in 1204. But a Roman state survived on the Bosporus until Ottoman artillery blasted its way through the Roman walls of Constantinople in 1453.

In the Middle East, however, a millennium of control by Greeks and Romans terminated and the region changed

Trapian silver, in unreconstructed state.
(National Museum of Scotland)

to leadership by a Semitic race. A visible sign was the reversion of many cities to their pre-Hellenistic local names – Urfa for Edessa, Membij for Hierapolis, Baalbek for Heliopolis, Amman for Philadelphia – the survival of Alexandria and Antioch (Antakya) were exceptional. The centre of gravity of the new power was also significant. For centuries the Romans had faced an eastern rival whose capitals lay in lower Mesopotamia and the Iranian plateau, whereas the new Arab Empire was usually based much closer to the Mediterranean world: in Syria under the Ummayads and Egypt under the Fatimids. Rome's Parthian and Sassanid enemies had rarely had access to the Mediterranean, whereas the Arabs occupied a number of major ports and rapidly developed a powerful navy. The Mediterranean ceased to be our sea, *mare nostrum*, and became an area of conflict and threat.

Arab control of North Africa extended this threat west, and initiated a structural divide between the northern and southern shores of the Mediterranean: whereas Roman Egypt and Africa had been tied closely into the Empire – socially, as the location of lucrative estates for the senatorial elite, and economically, as the major food providers for Rome and Constantinople – the Barbary Coast was a piratical scourge for Christian Europe. In Spain the Arabs remained the most powerful political force for 500 years, an object for crusade by the northern Christian enclaves but also a stimulus for intellectual and cultural fertilisation.

In north-western Europe Roman control ebbed most quickly and decisively. In the British Isles the Saxons gradually pushed the Romano-British into the far west and established their own competing kingdoms in much of England; the process contributed to the creation of popular stories of Arthur and strengthened ties between Cornwall and Brittany, but otherwise helped to confirm that Britain would develop separately from the continent. In France the consolidation of Pippinid or Carolingian control created the first post-Roman supranational political entity, the Holy Roman Empire, an institution which could challenge eastern Rome in terms of religious authority by manipulating the papacy and as true heirs to imperial Rome by the use of Latin and cultivation of Roman practices.

One area for competition between Holy Rome and eastern Rome was the Balkans, which long remained the most chaotic part of former Roman territory. Much had been overrun by groups of Slavs, but these had been slow to generate their own ruling elites. As Constantinople's power gradually revived in the eighth century, it proved possible to expand its authority in peninsular Greece and the south-eastern Balkans from the islands and coastal enclaves still in its possession, but large parts of the northern and north-western interior were ruled by whatever tribal group had managed to dominate the local Slavs and any survivors of the Roman population. The most important units to emerge were the Bulgar kingdom in the north-east, and the Serb and Croat kingdoms in the north-west. In each case the ruling elite developed a complex relationship with Constantinople, eager for the benefits (cultural as well as economic) of Roman recognition, but also wary of too close a dependence upon a potential imperial master. Constantinople's authority waxed and waned, and the best characterisation of the region is as a commonwealth: its members acknowledged strong ties, but there were also rivalries between potential rulers and the ruled, while the existence of alternative sources of support such as Holy Rome ensured that tensions thrived.

Slavs attempt to encourage the Avars to assist in an assault on Thessalonica (Miracles of St Demetrius §197).
'They said that all the cities and regions in its vicinity had been depopulated by them, and that it alone held out in their midst, while it had received all the refugees from the Danubian regions, and Pannonia, Dacia, Dardania and the remaining provinces and cities.'

Religious divisions

Competition for religious allegiance was one of the disrupting factors in the Balkans as Rome and Constantinople vied to convert different groups, and systems of belief are one of our major inheritances from the period of late-Roman warfare. The emergence of Christianity as a world faith was the first and most obvious, since it was through warfare that Christianity triumphed within the Empire. But the Roman Empire also shaped the nature of Christianity's development and helped to ensure that this universal religion existed in a variety of competing guises.

The struggle to define orthodoxy generated important excluded groups. In the fourth century Christians loosely associated with the views of Arius (that the Son was subordinate to the Father) had converted Germanic tribes north of the Danube. These tribes had remained unaffected by the final triumph within the Empire of Nicene over Arian Christianity in the 380s; as a result the successor kingdoms of Visigoths, Vandals and Ostrogoths all subscribed to Arian views and were regarded as heretical by Catholics.

In the east the identification in the 420s of the Nestorian heresy, over the status of the Virgin Mary and the place of the divine in Christ, had led to a rift: expulsion of Nestorians from the Empire had helped them to consolidate their domination in Sassanid Persia, where they became accepted as the national Church with their own spiritual leader, *catholicus*, whose appointment usually required royal sanction. Nestorian missionaries exploited Sassanid diplomatic and trading networks to make converts in India, central Asia and China. An inter-related dispute about Christ's nature generated the Monophysite schism in the eastern Empire from the mid-fifth century. Attempts at reconciliation failed, partly because doctrinal concessions to eastern Monophysites provoked disagreements with Rome and the western Church, partly because intermittent coercion served to harden attitudes; the textual bases for the arguments became swamped by propaganda, and their precise distinctions vanished because of the difficulty of translating complex arguments accurately between the languages involved – Latin, Greek, Coptic, Syriac, Armenian. In the mid-sixth century a separate Monophysite hierarchy of bishops emerged to control much of Egypt, Syria and Armenia. After the Arab conquests a new division of Christianity crys-talised, with the orthodox or Chalcedonians dominant within the Roman Empire, while Nestorians and Monophysites were the main groups in areas ruled by Arabs, where the limited numbers of Chalcedonians came to be known as Melkites, or emperors' men.

Inside the Empire Rome and Constantinople emerged as the two centres of religious power.

Doctrinal dissension almost generated civil war in the 340s, over the exile of Bishop Athanasius of Alexandria, and eastern attempts to resolve the Monophysite issue produced schisms in the late fifth, the mid-sixth, and for much of the seventh century. Successive emperors believed that they had the right to determine what was correct doctrine, and then the duty to see this accepted throughout their realm. Popes, whose independence was encouraged by Rome's decline as an imperial capital, saw themselves as the true guardians of Christian belief and relished occasions when eastern bishops appealed to the west for decisions. Emperors were prepared to use force to secure papal obedience, but this could only work if Rome itself was safely under eastern control. The basis for a split between Greek and Latin Christianity was established in late antiquity.

The church historian Evagrius laments the narrow disagreement between Chalcedonians ('in two natures') and Monopyhsites ('from two') which bitterly divided the Church (2.5).

'The envious and God-hating Devil thus wickedly devised and misinterpreted a change of a single letter, so that, whereas the utterance of one of these absolutely thereby introduces the other, by most people the difference is considered to be great and their meanings to be in outright antithetical opposition and to be exclusive of each other. For he who confesses Christ in two natures openly declares Him to be from two, in that by confessing Christ jointly in Divinity and humanity he declares in confessing that He is composed from Divinity and humanity.'

Christianity's triumph eliminated pagan beliefs at a formal level, but numerous pre-Christian practices were subsumed into the new religion in the process in spite of some condemnation. Christianity's secular power also caused contamination as episcopal office in the right city became a desirable route to power and wealth. The consequent dilution of the Christian message stimulated purists to seek a more authentic response to the Gospel: in different parts of the Empire individuals attempted to pursue a more rigorous regime, and some of these ascetics, or 'trainees', came to be organised into groups of monks. During the fourth century rules of conduct were developed in Egypt, Syria and Asia Minor and these soon spread west, so that by the time the Empire in the west was faltering in the mid-fifth century monasteries were sufficiently established to transmit Roman religious and cultural traditions.

Jews, however, were a victim of Christian zeal. In the pre-Christian Empire, Jews had usually been tolerated as an eccentric but acceptable group whose religious commitment was hallowed by antiquity, whereas for Christians they were the murderers of Christ. In the third-century persecutions, emperors had respected Jewish beliefs and not required sacrifice. In theory Jews continued to be protected by imperial legislation, but in practice this could not be upheld against enthusiastic Christian mobs: synagogues were destroyed, graveyards ransacked and congregations even forcibly converted. Such pressures produced a backlash and on occasions Jews sided with the Empire's enemies, most notoriously after the Persian siege of Jerusalem in 614. Suspicions against Jews increased and popular anti-Semitism came to be reinforced by official tolerance and legislation.

The other great religious change, generated by the wars of late antiquity, was Islam, which spread over the Near East and North Africa through armed conquest. Holy war, *jihad*, spurred expansion, while the privileged position of warriors in the early conquest communities in Iraq, Syria and Egypt, coupled with extra tax burdens on unbelievers, encouraged conversion. The Arab capture of Jerusalem and the Holy Land placed the sacred places of both Christians and Jews under alien authority and created a desire for retaliation. The east–west political rivalry of Sassanids and Romans had now been complicated by a potent religious factor.

Such far-reaching political and religious developments were accompanied by significant social and cultural changes. The corner-stone of the Roman Empire had been

S. Sophia (Hagia Sophia), Istanbul, Turkey. (Ancient Art and Architecture)

the city, which functioned as the centre for diffusing government, the religious focus for an area, and the social magnet for the local elite. In the same way as the growth of imperial prosperity was followed by the spread of urban institutions, so the retreat of Empire was accompanied by their shrinkage or disappearance. During the fourth and fifth centuries rural wealth and urban vitality had contracted away from the northern and western provinces, so that by the sixth century the most thriving cities were located in Asia Minor and Syria. The Arab conquests undermined urban institutions in those areas which remained under Roman control.

Paradoxically perhaps, cities continued to flourish under Arab authority as diverse, commercial social, and intellectual communities. By contrast, in the surviving Empire and the post-Roman west there had been a substantial fall in population levels, due to a combination of warfare, general insecurity, and disease. Bubonic plague had struck the Mediterranean in the 540s, and then returned with regularity for two

centuries. Population centres naturally suffered severely, since plague-bearing fleas needed a reasonable density of hosts in order to flourish; cities were particularly hard hit, but so were armies, and even rural areas such as Palestine (which supported a dense network of villages). For the rich, also, the obligations of urban life had already begun to outweigh the benefits. As a result cities became depopulated. In some areas, such as the north Balkans, there was a vertical move away from exposed lowland sites to the fortified hill-tops used by the pre-Roman inhabitants. Elsewhere the remnants of urban populations clustered around a place of refuge, perhaps a church or monastery, or a fortification built out of one of the massive remains of a Roman city such as a theatre or amphitheatre.

Cultural changes

These shrunken settlements were now dominated by their clergy, and perhaps a few powerful local families, but it was the Church, above all, which gave stability to these societies and determined their priorities. This is particularly evident in the case of education, which had been an important unifying badge for the elite of the Roman world. In the west monasteries became the guardians of knowledge as other sources of learning faded away, while in the east the clerical establishment in Constantinople provided the best opportunities for advanced study within the Empire.

As a result the balance of what was known inevitably shifted, with the priorities of the Church dominating: some aspects of the standard classical education in grammar and rhetoric survived, since clerics still had to participate in debates on doctrine and discipline, but the broad knowledge of the classical literary tradition possessed by leading writers in the fourth century had slipped, and the intellectual speculation encouraged by philosophical study also ceased. Of practical import was the decline in knowledge of languages, which meant that very few in the west outside Byzantine Italy could understand Greek and there were shortages of Latin speakers in the east. The intellectual centre of the Mediterranean world transferred to the lands conquered by Arabs: they ruled Alexandria, the most important university city of the Roman world, there was sufficient wealth in other cities to encourage families to finance the expense of higher education, and there was a curiosity to unlock the secrets of Hellenistic learning. Greek texts, especially of medicine, logic and philosophy, were translated into Arabic and studied, and in some cases it was the Islamic schools in Spain which acted as the conduit for the western rediscovery of this knowledge – Latin translations were made of Arabic versions of the Greek originals.

One aspect of ancient learning that continued to develop was law. In the 430s Theodosius II had presided over a major compilation of imperial law, and a century later Justinian had overhauled the law code and texts for legal education. Organised laws could contribute to the more effective exercise of power, and even the publication of a code bolstered authority. It is noticeable that rulers of post-Roman states in the West saw the advantages in publishing their own codes which combined Roman and Germanic law in differing proportions; this ensured that

important principles of Roman law were transmitted to medieval western kingdoms, and hence to serve as the base for much European law.

Diplomacy was another area of continuing development, driven by practical concerns. In the early Roman Empire there had been no tradition of systematic acquisition and compilation of information about neighbours and possible threats, but this had begun to change as the Empire came under increasing pressure. In the fifth century, when Attila's Huns were threatening the eastern Empire, Constantinople developed a system for regulating relations with Sassanid Persia in an effort to ensure stability, and also appreciated the advantages of detailed knowledge about other neighbours. In the sixth century these practices continued, so that eastern rulers were presented with information about the rulers of Axum in Ethiopia and the Turks in central Asia, all as part of Roman competition with Persia. The ability to play off possible enemies against each other became a hallmark of 'Byzantine' diplomacy, as the progressively weaker Empire relied more on non-military means to secure its survival.

Emperor Theodosius as a lawgiver. Frontispiece from Visigoth recension of the Codex of Theodosianus. (Ancient Art and Architecture)

Further reading

Bachrach, B.S., *Merovingian Military Organization 481–751*, Minneapolis (1972)

Barnwell, P.S., *Emperor, Prefects & Kings, the Roman West, 395–565*, London (1992)

Barnwell, P.S., *Kings, Courtiers and Imperium. The Barbarian West, AD 565–725*, London (1992)

Blockley, R.C., *The Fragmentary Classicising Historians of the Later Roman Empire II*, Cambridge (1985)

Blockley, R.C., *The History of Menander the Guardsman*, Cambridge (1985)

Blockley, R.C., *East Roman Foreign Policy, Formation and Conduct from Diocletian to Anastasius*, Cambridge (1992)

Bowersock, G.W., Brown, P., Grabar O., (eds.) *Late Antiquity, A Guide to the Postclassical World*, Cambridge, MA (1999)

Brown, P.R.L., *The World of Late Antiquity. From Marcus Aurelius to Muhammad*, London (1971)

Browning, R., *The Emperor Julian*, London (1975)

Burns, T.S., *A History of the Ostrogoths*, Bloomington (1984)

Bury, J.B., *History of the Later Roman Empire, from the death of Theodosius I to the death of Justinian* (1923)

Cameron, A., *Circus Factions, Blues and Greens at Rome and Byzantium*, Oxford (1976)

Cameron, A., & Long, J., *Barbarians and Politics at the Court of Arcadius*, Berkeley (1993)

Cameron, A.M., *Procopius and the Sixth Century*, London (1985)

Cameron, A.M., *The Later Roman Empire*, New York (1993)

Cameron, A.M., *The Mediterranean World in Late Antiquity*, London (1993)

Cameron, A.M., (ed.) *The Byzantine and Early Islamic Near East III, States, Resources, Armies*, Princeton (1995)

Cameron, A.M., & P. Garnsey (eds.) *The Cambridge Ancient History XIII AD 337–425*, Cambridge (1997)

Cameron, A.M., Ward-Perkins, B, & Whitby, L.M., (edd.) *The Cambridge Ancient History XIV AD 425–600*, Cambridge (2000)

Campbell, J.B., *The Emperor and the Roman Army 31 BC–AD 235*, Oxford (1984)

Collins, R., *Early Medieval Spain, Unity in Diversity 400–1000*, New York (1983)

Collins, R., *Early Medieval Europe, 300–1000*, London (1991)

Corcoran, S., *The Empire of the Tetrarchs, Imperial Pronouncements and Government AD 284–324*, Oxford (1996)

Cormack, R., *Writing in Gold: Byzantine Society and its Icons*, London (1985)

Crump, G., *Ammianus Marcellinus as a Military Historian*, Wiesbaden (1975)

Dodgeon, M.H., & Lieu, S.N.C., *The Roman Eastern Frontier and the Persian Wars, AD 226–363*, London (1991)

Donner, F., *Early Islamic Conquests*, Princeton (1981)

Drinkwater, J., & Elton H., (edd.) *Fifth-century Gaul: a Crisis of Identity?*, Cambridge (1992)

Evans, J.A.S., *The Age of Justinian, the Circumstances of Imperial Power*, London (1996)

Ferrill, A., *The Fall of the Roman Empire, the Military Explanation*, London (1986)

Fowden, G., *Empire to Commonwealth, Consequences of Monotheism in Late Antiquity*, Princeton (1993)

Frank, R.I., *Scholae Palatinae: the Palace Guards of the Later Roman Empire*, Rome (1969)

Garnsey, P., & Humfress, C., *The Evolution of the Late Antique World*, Cambridge (2001)

Goffart, W., *Barbarians and Romans AD 418–584: The Techniques of Accommodation*, Princeton (1980)

Greatrex, G., *Rome and Persia at War, 502–532*, Leeds (1998)

Greatrex, G., & S.N.C. Lieu, *The Roman Eastern Frontier and the Persian Wars II, AD 363–630*, London (2002)

Haldon, J.F., *Recruitment and Conscription in the Byzantine Army c.550–950*, Vienna (1979)

Haldon, J.F., *Byzantium in the Seventh Century, the Transformation of a Culture*, Cambridge (1990)

Harries, J., *Sidonius Apollinaris and the Fall of Rome*, Oxford (1994)

Heather, P.J., *Goths and Romans 332–489*, Oxford (1991)

Heather, P.J., *The Goths*, Oxford (1996)

Holum, K., *Theodosian Empresses: Women and Imperial Dominion in Late Antiquity*, Berkeley (1982)

Isaac, B., *The Limits of Empire, The Roman Army in the East*, Oxford (1990)

James, E., *The Origins of France: from Clovis to the Capetians 500–1000*, London (1983)

James, E., *The Franks*, Oxford (1988)

Jones, A.H.M., *The Later Roman Empire 284–602, A Social, Economic and Administrative Survey*, Oxford (1964)

Jones, A.H.M., Martindale, J.R., & Morris, J., (eds.) *The Prosopography of the Later Roman Empire I*, Oxford (1971)

Kaegi, W.E., *Byzantine Military Unrest, 471–843: An Interpretation*, Amsterdam (1981)

Kaegi, W.E., *Byzantium and the Early Islamic Conquests*, Cambridge (1992)

Lee, A.D., *Information and Frontiers, Roman foreign relations in late antiquity*, Cambridge (1993)

Liebeschuetz, J.H.W.G., *Barbarians and Bishops, Army, Church and State in the Age of Arcadius and John Chrysostom*, Oxford (1990)

Luttwak, E.N., *The Grand Strategy of the Roman Empire from the First Century AD to the Third*, Baltimore (1976)

MacMullen, R., *Soldier and Civilian in the Later Roman Empire*, Cambridge, MA (1963)

MacMullen, R., *Corruption and the Decline of Rome*, New Haven (1988)

McCormick, M., *Eternal Victory, Triumphal Rulership in Late Antiquity, Byzantium and the Early Medieval West*, Cambridge (1986)

Mango, C.A., *Byzantium: The Empire of New Rome*, London (1980)

Martindale, J.R.(ed.), *The Prosopography of the Later Roman Empire II–III*, Cambridge (1980, 1992)

Matthews, J.F., *Western Aristocracies and Imperial Court AD 364–425*, Oxford (1975)

Millar, F., *The Roman Near East, 31 BC – AD 337*, Cambridge, MA (1993)

Moorhead, J., *Theoderic in Italy*, Oxford (1992)

Nicasie, M.J., *Twilight of Empire: the Roman Army from the Reign of Diocletian until the Battle of Adrianople*, Amsterdam (1998)

Nixon, C.E.V., & Rodgers, B.S., *In Praise of Later Roman Emperors, The* Panegyrici Latini, Berkeley (1994)

Obolensky, D., *The Byzantine Commonwealth*, London (1971)

O'Flynn, J.M., *Generalissimos of the Western Roman Empire*, Edmonton (1983)

Rich, J., and Shipley, G., *War and Society in the Roman World*, London (1993)

Southern,P., & Dixon, K.R., *The Late Roman Army*, London (1996)

Thompson, E.A., *Romans and Barbarians, the decline of the Western Empire*, Madison (1982)

Thompson, E.A., *The Huns*, Oxford (1995)

Treadgold, W., *The Byzantine Army*, Stanford (1995)

Treadgold, W., *A History of the Byzantine State and Society*, Stanford (1997)

Van Dam, R., *Leadership and Community in Late Antique Gaul*, Berkeley (1985)

Watson, A., *Aurelian and the Third Century*, London (1999)

Whitby, L.M., *The Emperor Maurice and His Historian, Theophylact Simocatta on Persian and Balkan Warfare*, Oxford (1988)

Whittaker, C.R., *Frontiers of the Roman Empire, a Social and Economic Study*, Baltimore (1994)

Whittow, M., *The Making of Orthodox Byzantium, 600–1025*, London (1996)

Wickham, C., *Early Medieval Italy, Central Power and Local Society 400–1000*, London (1981)

Williams, S., *Diocletian and the Roman Recovery*, London (1985)

Williams, S., & Friell, G., *The Rome That Did Not Fall: the survival of the East in the Fifth Century*, London (1999)

Wolfram, H., *History of the Goths*, Berkeley (1988)

Wood, I.N., *The Merovingian Kingdoms, 450–751*, Harlow (1994)

Index

Related titles from Osprey Publishing

To order any of these titles, or for more information on Osprey Publishing, contact:

Osprey Direct (UK) *Tel:* +44 (0)1933 443863 *Fax:* +44 (0)1933 443849 *E-mail:* info@ospreydirect.co.uk

Osprey Direct (USA) c/o MBI Publishing *Toll-free:* 1 800 826 6600 *Phone:* 1 715 294 3345

Fax: 1 715 294 4448 *E-mail:* info@ospreydirectusa.com

www.ospreypublishing.com

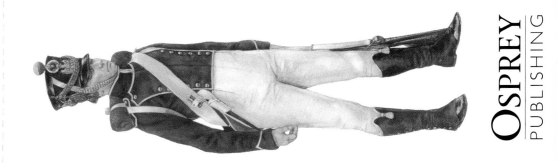

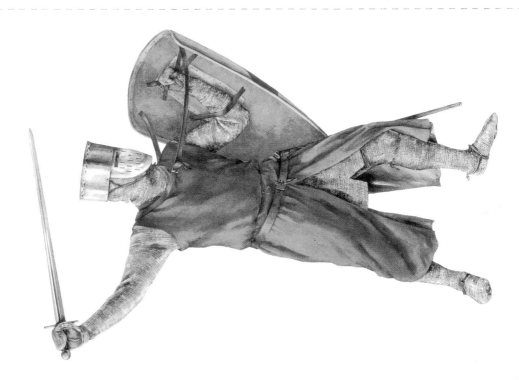

OSPREY
PUBLISHING

www.ospreypublishing.com

call our telephone hotline
for a free information pack

USA & Canada: 1-800-826-6600
UK, Europe and rest of world call:
+44 (0) 1933 443 863

Young Guardsman
Figure taken from *Warrior 22:
Imperial Guardsman 1799–1815*
Published by Osprey
Illustrated by Christa Hook

Knight, c.1190
Figure taken from *Warrior 1: Norman Knight 950 – 1204AD*
Published by Osprey
Illustrated by Christa Hook

POSTCARD